WHY DIDN'T I DIE

WHY DIDN'T I DIE

A Memoir of PTSD

F. W. KIRKPATRICK

STUDIO
OF BOOKS
THE SPACE FOR YOUR MESSAGE

Studio of Books LLC
5900 Balcones Drive Suite 100
Austin, Texas 78731
www. studioofbooks. org
Hotline: (254) 800-1183

Ordering Information:
Special discounts are available on quantity purchases by corporations, associations, and others. For details, contact the publisher at the address above.

Printed in the United States of America.

ISBN-13: Softcover   978-1-964148-11-3
         Hardcover   978-1-964148-12-0
         eBook   978-1-964148-13-7

Library of Congress Control Number: 2024906610

CONTENTS

Prologue i

CHAPTER 1

A State of Madness. 1

CHAPTER 2

A Normal Life. 14

CHAPTER 3

Welcome to South Vietnam. 29

CHAPTER 4

A Slaughter is Coming 38

CHAPTER 5

The Battle of Ong Thanh 61

CHAPTER 6

The Return from Japan. .96

CHAPTER 7

That's Impossible 105

CHAPTER 8

The Boys Are Back 115

CHAPTER 9

The Return to Normal 131

CHAPTER 10

Struggling to be Normal.......................138

CHAPTER 11

From Good to Horrible 144

CHAPTER 12

Ward 13.....................................151

CHAPTER 13

Retirement...................................174

EPILOGUE 189

Author's Note 201

Appendix A

Statistical Summary of
The Battle of Ong Thanh 202

Appendix B

Unit History of 2nd
Battalion 28th Infantry.......................204

Appendix C

59 soldiers Killed in Action
as a result of the Battle of Ong Thanh..........206

Appendix D

Presumptive Conditions
for Agent Orange. 210

Appendix E

Neurological and Psychiatric Symptoms of
Agent Orange. 213

Appendix F

PTSD Checklist 215

Prologue

Sometime in 2007, I was at a bar with a bunch of 30-year-olds. One of them, a navy commander, was on leave from his naval assignment in San Diego, California. I mentioned that I was a Vietnam Veteran and started talking about a battle in Vietnam that happened before he was born. He replied, "That's boring. No one is interested in Vietnam."

He probably would not understand how the children of the "Greatest Generation", would come home from Vietnam as symbols of "the only war the United States ever lost." He probably would not understand the psychological effects of coming home from war to rejection, criticism, and anti-war protestors chants of "losers, baby-killers." And I doubt if he would understand why this "old dinosaur" is still haunted by the names Johnson, Lincoln, Megiveron, Peters, Reece, Tizzio, and Wilson.

When I came home from combat in 1968 from Vietnam, friends said that I was still the same. But inner turmoil was eating at my mind and screamed, "I'm not the same." The turmoil was affecting me and everyone around me, but I was powerless to change my actions because I did not understand what was happening to me for nearly twenty years.

After my return from Vietnam, my legacy for the next forty years was drug abuse, alcoholism, bipolar disorder, hyper vigilance, violent behavior, significant employment problems, survivor guilt, flashbacks, major gaps in memory, relationship issues, depression, anxiety attacks, bursts of unwarranted anger, paranoia, a suicide attempt, and a ten-day commitment to a mental institution.

It was not until 1980, that the term PTSD that defined my legacy came to be known. The term Post Traumatic Stress Disorder (PTSD) was not officially recognized as a mental health condition until 1980, a full twelve years after I left Vietnam. The term PTSD became a household name after the release of the third edition of the Diagnostic and Statistical Manual of Mental Disorders (DSM-III) and is associated with the legacy of the Vietnam War.

(PTSD - A condition of persistent mental and emotional stress occurring because of injury or severe psychological shock.) [1]

The Effects of Post-Traumatic Stress Disorder on someone's life leaves almost nothing unchanged. The longer that PTSD exists without treatment, the greater the effects of PTSD on a person's life. [2]

Here is a sample of how PTSD affected my life:

- *Paranoia* - Many times I felt threats to my life when there were none.

- *Relationships* - I was cold, distant, and unable to form close, interpersonal relationships. I had an intense fear of closeness. I live alone now and don't see myself with anyone in the future.

- *Dissociative Amnesia* - I have major gaps in my memory and am confused or unsure about certain events that happened in Vietnam.

---

1   American Psychiatric Association, "What is Post Traumatic Stress Disorder.", http://www. psychiatry. org/patients-families/ptsd/what-is-ptsd

2   The Refuge, "PTSD: Statistics, Causes, Signs, & Symptoms - https://www. therefuge-ahealingplace. com/ptsd-treatment/effects-symptoms-signs/

- *Bursts of Anger* - Explosions of out-of-control rage was common for me.

- *Survivor Guilt* - I believed I did something wrong when I survived death while my friends did not.

- *Sleep Problems* - I have not slept well since I returned from Vietnam. I have problems falling asleep at night and usually only sleep for a few hours at a time.

- *Substance Abuse* - Alcoholism and drug use for four years after my return from Vietnam.

- *Suicidal Thoughts* - Thoughts like that would come and go several times in my life.

- *Significant Employment Problems* - Almost my entire life I had an extremely hard time holding on to a job for any period.

- *Anxiety Attacks* - Certain conditions made me think I was going to die, even when there was no danger. I feared for those close to me, that something bad was going to happen to them, even when there was no threat. I had an intense fear of certain events like snow and fireworks. Driving over bridges, high above the ground, terrified me.

- *Personality Disorder* - I was obsessed with killing among a range of other unstable problems.

- *Hyper Vigilance* - I was always on guard, especially at night. I could not sleep normally because I feared for my life if I fell asleep. I got up every few hours to check that no one was near my house.

- *Flashbacks* - I believed I was back in Vietnam in mortal danger, even though I was safely home in my own bed. The feeling was very real to me.

- *Nightmares* - I had weird dreams that were almost always about death or killing.

- *Depression* - I felt sad much of the time and did not like to do many things. I could not concentrate because my mind was always wandering.

Related Effects of PTSD on Other Problems I Experienced:

1. Bipolar Disorder - Having PTSD along with bipolar disorder, makes the bipolar disorder worse and creates greater levels of depression. [3]

2. Type 2 Diabetes - People suffering from PTSD have a significant risk of developing type 2 Diabetes. [4]

3. Agent Orange Exposure - Veterans exposed to Agent Orange had more comorbidities including diabetes, hypertension, cerebrovascular disease, depression, and PTSD. [5]

4. Tinnitus - I have this constant swirling sound in my right ear that I hear mostly at night. My constant exposure to gunfire and explosions while in Vietnam, may have caused tinnitus.

The difference between PTSD and almost all other psychiatric disorders, is that there is a historical event that sets this off. [6] For me, that event occurred on October 17, 1967, a date that is forever seared in my mind and will NEVER go away:

On June 25, 1876, General George Armstrong Custer, suffered a severe defeat at the Battle of the Little Bighorn, commonly referred to as Custer's Last Stand. Five of the 7th Calvary's twelve companies were annihilated,

---

3   The Effect of PTSD on People with Bipolar Disorder, Matthew Tull, PhD, https://www. verywellmind. com/the-effect-of-ptsd-and-bipolar-disorder-2797517

4   PTSD associated with type 2 diabetes - https://www. sciencedaily. com/ releases/2013/05/130516063839. htm

5   Agent Orange Plus PTSD Equals Extra Dementia Risk - https://www. medpagetoday. com/meetingcoverage/aaic/52698

6   The Soldier's Heart, Dr. Matthew Friedman - https://www. pbs. org/wgbh/ pages/frontline/shows/heart/themes/ptsd. html

one Crow Scout, who left early did survive, as well as a lone horse. There were 210 U. S. casualties, including General George Custer. It was a major battlefield blunder. At that time, it was the worst American military disaster ever. [7]

Not as well-known as the Battle of the Bighorn, the Battle of Ong Thanh that happened on October 17, 1967, in South Vietnam, was a slaughter that equaled the Suicide charge of the Light Brigade and Custer's Last Stand.

---

7   What Really Happened at Custer's Last Stand? - Annette McDermott, https://www. history. com/news/what-really-happened-at-custers-last-stand

CHAPTER 1

A State of Madness

(March 2005)

I am hearing scratching and crawling noises that stop and start again. Now the sounds are of moaning and groaning that are getting closer and closer to me. The faint cry of, "Fred, help me", startles me out of a deep sleep.

I have been here for two weeks and even at 1a. m, it is unusually quiet on Ward 13. Only the two psych nurses on duty at their Nurse's Station, are up at this weird hour. That is until yelling comes from the nearby dayroom from patients who are also up.

Arriving at the dayroom, I expect to see familiar faces, but find an unfamiliar crowd of six with name tags on their PJ's. They all look to be near my age of sixty, except for Willie C Johnson. who looks slightly older?

Willie C Johnson and Wilbert Peters are both black men. Kenneth Wilson, freckle-faced with reddish blond hair, is taller than anyone at six feet tall. Ronnie Reece is handsome with light brown hair. Emil Megiveron has the look of a Native American, while Pasquale Tizzio, built like a linebacker, has the dark features of an Italian.

None of them are smiling and have that sad look of depression that I have known for so many years.

Willie C. , who appears to be the leader, is yelling at them in his Southern accent. "All moanin I've been hearn y'all say I ain't never gonna do that. Why Sheeit that is un-American." Suddenly, Willie C. sees me and focuses his attention on me.

He says, "Kirkpatrick, did y'all have fun in Jay Pan. Now cause of y'all, I ain't never gonna see my Barbara.

Emil Megiveron says, "And I'm never going to talk with my sister Mary in Pontiac."

Ronney Reece is having trouble speaking and starts stuttering, "W-W-Why did y'all take my vacation. I ain't never gonna see Ad Lanna no more."

Wilbert Peters is yelling at me, "Why'd y'all give me that their bed. Now I ain't got a head no more."

Kenneth Wilson says, "Aah recon y'all yankee dudden did no good by us all."

Pasquale Tizzio, the last to speak, "Kirkpatrick, I told you I ain't doin it, but you tawked and said your goin to get outta here by taking that job."

I said to all of them, "How do you know my name? I don't know any of you or what you are talking about."

They all fire back, "Yes you do know who we are. You left us all alone out there. And now were all dead."

I'm screaming back at them, "It wasn't my fault. They made me leave", unaware that I'm screaming, till I hear, "Kirkpatrick, Kirkpatrick, wake up."

A psych nurse is shaking me, trying to bring me out of a deep sleep. I wake up. My pulse is racing. My blood pressure is sky high. My heart is about to explode.

"Where are all the guys with the name tags?" I yell.

She says, "You know we don't allow anyone to have name tags for privacy reasons."

I continue, "But I saw them in the dayroom, and they were wearing name tags."

She says, "I was just at the Dayroom, and no one is there. You were just having a bad nightmare."

After nearly forty years of struggling with PTSD, I am exhausted and want to give up.

(1968-1971)

Some of my closest friends said I was still the same and had not changed much, that I was normal. But I wonder if they would think me normal if I told them some of what I saw:

The corpse of the dead VC is holding a mortar tube in his hands. From the waist up, his body is gone. His head is missing.

Some soldier digs up a skull from sacred VC burial grounds, mounts it on a stake and put a unit patch, or the Ace of Spades, on top of the skull.

Some soldiers are wearing necklaces of dead VC ears, cut off as souvenirs of kills made.

A VC is thrown out of a helicopter, high above the ground, for not telling them what they wanted.

I am experiencing many physical problems:

Aches and pains, even when I am not doing anything strenuous. A swirling sound in my right ear that never goes away, and the sound gets much worse at night. Horrible headaches that feel like my head is about to explode. My back pain is so severe, I can hardly walk.

The first few weeks at home, people from the neighborhood ask me questions about Vietnam. The number one question was always, "How many VC did you Kill?" My answer was always the same, "I don't know", and quickly change the subject.

I tell them about ambush patrols, setup to provide early warning, that was a potential suicide if things went bad.

How we did not sleep all night. How we slept in a small circle in extremely uncomfortable positions with no bed, no pillow, and only a small blanket to keep the mosquitoes off that tried to bite you all night, or to keep you warm from the rain or cold damp night.

If it rained, you slept in the mud, and it was much harder to hear noises. I told them you rarely ever saw the dead bodies of the Viet Cong; you only knew by the smells of dead bodies that were taken away by the VC.

The bloody mess of dead animals on the streets, makes me sick to my stomach. The awful stench of decaying flesh, like Cleveland's slaughterhouses that kills cows, takes me back to Vietnam and that unforgettable smell of dead VC bodies.

Reading, which was always such a pleasure for me, is no longer possible. I read a sentence and my mind goes blank. I drift into the world of la-la land and remember nothing. I become frustrated as my mind wanders. I try to re-read, but the results are the same and I give up.

There are many dreams and nightmares. Several times a week, I experience terror and visit death close again. I wake up in a cold sweat, screaming and shaking, as I come out of a bad dream.

I am certain that I will never forget what they are about, but when I wake up, I have a hard time remembering but a few of them:

In one nightmare, I wake up screaming, "Get down or they'll kill you." My heart is racing, my skin soaked. I am shaking violently, and my chest is so tight that I can barely breathe.

In another dream, I am screaming, "Come get me you bastards, I'm gonna kill all of you", as I wake up trembling, shaking, sweating, and gasping for air since I had just escaped death.

One dream was very bizarre and disturbing. It must have happened in Vietnam:

I am crawling in a dark tunnel and come across bodies suspended in the air above my head. They are hanging from large human hooks, pierced into their skin. They are moaning in pain. I look up to see their faces but find there are no heads attached to the bodies.

Some nights I have the same two contrasting dreams:

In the first dream, I am in a foxhole with a machine gun. I am being attacked by row-after-row of enemy soldiers. I mow them down, killing hundreds at a time. All the while, they are getting closer and closer to my foxhole. I am on my last rounds of ammo, surrounded, and about to be killed. I fight to wake up to save my life.

The second dream feels even more real, as if it were something that had happened. I am walking point in front of my company, and suddenly I am under fire. I hear the rounds and stop, frozen in time. The rest of my company is moving forward as I'm cowering in fear, holding my rosary that is around my neck. One of the guys comes up to me and asks,

"What's wrong?" I say, "They're trying to kill me."

Except, there is no shooting. I have just imagined everything, except for the fear. I wake up screaming and yelling.

There are days when things are moving faster than I can keep up:

Turmoil is eating the inside of my head. My mind is ready to explode. My thoughts are moving too fast.

I cannot concentrate on what my date is saying. I struggle to keep up with her words.

Things are happening. Things are moving fast. I do not want to go to the hospital. But I might black out. Insurance is not enough. I do not know. Not sure. What should I do today? Wonder what is on today. I told him. "Get Out." What time is it. Is it eight? So let me know. I cannot. Are you going?

I say to her, "What did you say? "

She says, "Shh! You are talking so loudly. Why are you yelling."

I say, " I didn't know what you're talking about."

She says, "Stop Yelling."

I said, "I'm not yelling. THIS IS YELLING."

And other days, I am so tired:

I felt so exhausted. I dread talking with anyone. I rarely go out or answer my phone. My dirty dishes have been piling up in the kitchen sink for weeks. I am too fatigued to wash them. Eating exhausts me. Some days, I sit in my chair for hours, too tired to move or talk. My deep depression is draining my energy. Thinking makes my head hurt. Life seems hopeless. I am sad and gloomy. Nothing gave me pleasure. I do not want to get out of bed.

The feeling of constant danger is always at my side. I fear everything, and I rarely leave the safety of my home:

I grew up driving in some of Cleveland's worst driving conditions. But now, even reports of snow falling creates anxiety and fear for me. Driving is so scary now. My pulse is racing, I'm shaking and sweating so bad as I drive, I think I'm having a heart attack. I feel like my life is in constant danger. I had to call off work several times when the threat of moderate snow made me want to throw up.

The drive over to Jimmy's house, that early afternoon in August 1968, went from peaceful to terrifying. I was doing fine until I started crossing over a bridge high above the valley. As soon as I see the tops of trees, I have this sudden fear of driving off the bridge. I am light-headed, dizzy, and my heart is beating so fast I think it will explode.

I feel trapped in my car and want to stop and get out of the car but cannot because cars are behind me. I look away from the treetops and move cautiously away from the outside lane. And just like that, the threat is over, and I am on the other side of the bridge.

I finally arrive on Jimmy's street and start walking on the sidewalk towards his house. I am less than a block from his house when I see danger in front of me. Three young men are walking towards me on the same side of the street. As they get closer, I see their fists clenched in a street-fighting fashion. They look menacing and extremely dangerous to me. I am trembling in fear. I am fearful for my life. I am wishing I had my M-16 rifle so I could kill them before they get any closer. I am shaking violently as they are almost on top of me. I realize now that I am going to have to fight for my life.

I fear that if I get into a fistfight, I will be beaten to death. I will have to kill at least one of them quickly for a chance of survival. I am also considering crossing the street. Before I can decide, I hear a familiar voice,

"Hey Fred, welcome back from Vietnam. We thought you might like to experience some danger again." It is my friend Jimmy and two other friends. They are all laughing not knowing that I would have killed all three of them if I had my rifle. I do not think Jimmy understands that I no longer am willing to face danger again.

I am now aware of many sounds I never used to notice. Loud noises, such as doors slamming or fireworks, startle me, and my body shakes in fear of the unknown. If I am sleeping, any sudden noise or movement quickly brings me out of even the deepest slumber.

Nights are the most perilous time of the day for me. I now have a childlike fear of darkness. It terrifies me because I cannot see what is out there. Darkness used to signal that it was time to sleep, but no more. I toss and turn, unable to sleep. Sleep avoids me as I lay awake at night for hours, exhausted, afraid to sleep, thinking I will not wake up alive. When exhaustion finally overtakes me, I wake up most nights in a deep sweat, as constant nightmares invade my sleep.

The demons that lay within me will not let me go into peaceful sleep. With darkness outside, comes constant danger everywhere. I fear for my life from people I do not know, thinking they will kill me.

On a trip to Las Vegas, I go out on a dark late night and wander too far from my hotel onto an unfamiliar street. With strangers in front of me, I quickly cross the street to avoid them. I am shaking violently. I fear they want to harm me, that my life is in grave danger, yet no one is trying to harm me.

I am angry at anything and anyone. I succumb to violent fits of rage and anger for no good reason. Several incidents in late 1968 made me wonder if I was mentally unstable or only plain violent and insane.

In late September 1968, I visit the Hot Dog Inn with my friend Ray. The Hot Dog Inn had great hot dogs, but is in a seedy part of Cleveland, with mostly dangerous clientele. As I am in line getting ready to place my order, some drunk guy bumps into me and knocks the change from my hands. Normally this would not bother me, but today is different.

I explode into a violent rage, yelling, "Watch where you're going asshole."

Quickly four of his friends jump to his defense and an all-out brawl is about to happen. As they start to surround me and Ray, I scream at the top of my lings, "What a dumbass you are. You are dumber than shit. You wouldn't last a day in combat."

My friend Ray pretends he has a gun in his coat. Pointing the fake gun at them, he yells, "Back off." His ploy works and we leave but my blood pressure is sky high.

A month later, Ray and his cousin meet me at a bowling alley on Saturday. We plan to bowl several games and have a few beers. After we are done bowling, we are sitting down drinking beer from a plastic cup. It is a few minutes before midnight. The night manager comes up to us and says he needs us to finish the beers before midnight because they don't have a Sunday license.

I was about half-way done with my beer and in no hurry to finish it. I said to the manager, "I will give you this cup when I'm done with it."

This caused the manger to say to me, "No, I need your cup now."

This sets me off and I am screaming at him, "You want this beer, come take it out of my hands."

The manager walks towards me, and I jump quickly to my feet. My friend Ray gets in-between us and by that time I have finished my beer.

There were many other incidents in the next few years. Sometimes I can go for weeks being normal, but then something would set me off like a firecracker.

Suddenly with no reason, I would go off on someone, yelling and screaming,

"Bastards, Fuck You, Stupid mother fuckers" with insane rages and fits of anger.

I would think later when I was calm again, "Why am I completely out of control? When did it I become so crazy? When did it happen that I'm now so abnormal from anyone else?"

In those moments when I in a violent rage, I am irrational and unpredictable. I have no control over my actions and can do anything. I have so much hatred inside of me and I do not understand why.

Street Racing, on the streets of Cleveland gives me the adrenaline rush I need. I am pushing myself to dangerous extreme speeds of nearly 100 mph. But twice, this dangerous sport almost ended tragically:

During one of these races, I was on the outside and my competitor was on the inside. As usual, I got the early lead and was well out in front. However, I see a car in front of me parked on the inside lane.

My competitor is on a collision course with the parked car. He is trapped. He could not stop in time since I have him boxed in. I hit hard on my brakes. My grateful challenger waves his hand, a thank you motion, as I let him pass in front of me.

Another time, I was racing and went past a police speed trap. I knew that a chase car would be waiting for me. I am planning to slow down and stop, but I hit a hill and my car goes airborne. A police officer jumps in front of me and signals for me to pull over. I struggle to stop. He thinks I am trying to get away and reaches for his gun to shoot me. I just barely miss hitting him as I come to a complete stop.

My drinking had started slowly in the Army, a beer or two once a week, and then grew to binge drinking once a month in Vietnam to help me forget some of what I saw. By the time I am discharged from the Army in August 1968, the drinking has become much worse.

I am drinking eight or more mixed drinks daily. I like the taste and feeling, but I am developing a lethal addiction to alcohol and my mind is slowly deteriorating. Alcohol is no longer helping with my issues, so I'm seeking another form of relief.

I start my experiment with two new forms of drugs called Barbiturates and Amphetamines.

Barbiturates are drugs that acts as a system depressant and can affect you from mild sedation to total anesthesia. Taking the wrong dose could lead to death. People on the street call them "downers" or "reds" because the pill is red. I find them unhelpful since they knock you out for hours and do not produce the feeling I want.

One Saturday night, a few of us took them to sleep. We were laying on the floor with the radio playing rock-n-roll music. When I woke up Sunday morning, the station was playing church sermons. Even though I was only inches from the radio knob, I was not able to change the station. I tried to talk to the others asleep next to me, but my words were slow and slurred as if in a drunken state.

Amphetamines work on the central nervous system. On the street they are known as "speed", "uppers" or "yellows" for the color of the pill. The feeling is mind blowing. One time after taking them, I was up for two straight days, which was great for those two-day card games we played. We would be in a constant state of movement with rapid fire conversations at the speed of light. I kept moving my jaw up and down to relax from the jitters and trembling. Eating food was impossible.

I try LSD, more commonly known as "acid", once at a nightclub. Within an hour, I am in a weird state where nothing seemed normal. The sounds are everywhere but I cannot understand any of the words. And then my mind starts to play tricks on me.

At a bowling alley, I see guys throwing themselves down the bowling alley at the bowling pins. I got a little freaky when I imagined a group talking about:

"Hey, those guys are high on acid, let's call the police on them." I am freaked out and ready to run out of the bowling alley. I tell our "trip guide" and he tells me it's my imagination and the incident passes.

I go into the bathroom and look in the mirror. I keep looking into the mirror and my face turns into a monster mask with parts falling out. I fight to turn away from the mirror and walk outside. I was glad when the trip finally ended and was able to return to "normal".

By the beginning of 1971, I have stopped taking drugs and rarely drinking. I am convinced that I am getting back to normal, but two events in 1971 changed my mind:

Early 1971, I report for work on the midnight shift at the Ford Motor Company. After about an hour, our line is shut down and we are told we were being transferred from the Core Room to the hated Foundry Room.

The Foundry Room is such a dirty and foul place that many who worked that line would call off sick weekly. This had been going on for months and other lines would be shut down since the Foundry room would not have enough workers to run this very essential line. This was the third time this month that I was being transferred to the Foundry Room.

Today I was determined to fight management at all costs.

The Foundry Room was the most important part of the operation at the Ford Motor Company Casting Plant. Dirt modes on wheels, on the assembly line, required that each worker "gently" place sand parts into open holes that corresponded to the dirt sample.

Once this process was completed, the mold moved, and hot melted steel was poured on the mold. This causes them to "harden" and form engine parts. They were then removed and sent to the Engine Plant to be cleaned and put into an engine.

I knew exactly what this job required since I had done it several times before. This time, I would have none of this. I was determined to shut the line down completely. As the dirt molds came up to me, I would "throw" the sand parts into the mold. This would effectively destroy the dirt mold and they would have to be scrapped.

After about 30 minutes of me destroying production, the line was shutdown. Shutting down a line at Ford Motor Company, even for a minute, is rarely ever done.

In a few minutes, "The Man in the White Hat", is heading straight for me. I know exactly who he is. He is the top man in the foundry known as "The Superintendent". Only bad things happen when he shows up. All foremen fear him because he can fire any of them for any reason in an instant.

The Superintendent rushes over to confront me. He is yelling at me,

"What the fuck are you doing. You have destroyed millions of dollars of production."

I confront him by yelling back, "Who the fuck are you?"

This really sets him off and he yells, "I'm the Superintendent and you are about to be fired." I say to him in a calm voice, "For what. No one ever told me how to do this job."

My logic wins over the Superintendents logic. He has someone show me how to do the job properly. I have now calmed down and am working like everyone else.

But just before our shift ends, I am bringing parts over on this heavy rack. The rack gets caught on the pulling assembly. I tried to pull it free but cannot. Just about that time, a foreman comes along, and the rack flips over. I am blamed for deliberately pushing the cart into the line, destroying property, and taken to the office where I was quickly fired.

The second event was far more troubling. It made me think, "Was I devoid of empathy and remorse? Was I becoming too dangerous for society?"

Why would a good Catholic boy who wanted to be an altar boy, who sang in the church choir, and who loved to attend Sunday mass, want to kill three men in cold blood with a high-powered rifle?

June 3, 1971

It has taken nearly a month of planning, but now these three scumbags will have the life drained out of them. The first-round hits scumbag#1 in the head and his head explodes into dust. Scumbag#2 takes a round to where his genitals used to be just a few seconds ago. As the leader of the group, scumbag#3 will suffer before he begs to die. Round one blows off his left kneecap. Round two takes his right kneecap off. He yells in pain and tries to crawl away. The third-round separates most of his left shoulder from his body. The fourth-round hits just below his buttocks and he flips over. The fifth-round hits the middle of his throat and finishes the job.

Happy Birthday Fred!

CHAPTER 2

A Normal Life

(1947-1966)

Guatemala in May 1956 is controlled by cruel military dictator, President Carlos Castillo Armas. But that did not deter my mother from taking my two brothers and I to Guatemala for the birth of my sister. In July 1956, police crackdown on college protesters, at a rally against Armas's abuse of power. They kill one student and arrest over 200 others, many of them are gravely wounded.

One of those protesters is my uncle Edward. He was able to narrowly escape arrest that morning by hiding at my grandmother's house. But by early afternoon, there was a banging on the door, "Policia, Abre la puerta ahora." Three army soldiers, with automatic weapons, search the house and arrest my uncle. His arrest lasts a week but left a life-long impression on this nine-year-old.

President Carlos Castillo Armas, the 28th president of Guatemala, served from 1954 to 1957, taking power in a coup d'état. Soon after taking power, he put down a coup from young army cadets, leaving 29 of them dead and another 91 wounded.

He cracked down on unions and peasant organizations, arresting many thousands of opposition leaders, branding them communists, and killing thousands. Armas was shot dead on July 26, 1957, by a member of the presidential guard. [8]

Early Monday morning, October 1, 1956, my father takes me to see President Eisenhower, during his visit to our hometown of Cleveland, Ohio. We walked nearly three miles from our apartment in the low-income projects on the lower Westside, to the corner of Detroit and West 25th street. My father wants to get a great view as we wait for the Presidential motorcade.

We were at least an hour early, yet the crowds were already lined up on both sides of the street. Within the hour, the crowds are in the thousands. Our wait pays off. A police motorcycle is leading the way to clear the way and block traffic. Armored vehicles are soon followed by twenty to thirty vehicles from the motorcade. President Eisenhower, in a big black open Lincoln convertible, is dressed in what looks like a tuxedo.

He is sitting in the convertible, but when he sees the huge crowd, he is on his feet, waving with one hand as he tips his big black Top Hat to the crowd. The motorcade, traveling at a terribly slow speed, is on its way to downtown Cleveland for a rally on Public Square during his presidential campaign. It was something that this nine-year-old will never forgot.

I have been born many years earlier in June of 1947, to my perfectly mismatched parents, Bill and Aida Kirkpatrick in Cleveland, Ohio. I often wondered how they met. Was it love at first sight or just an arranged marriage? My mother, an extremely attractive woman, is 23 years old when I was born. She has beautiful brown hair and beautiful skin and likes to say she is 5' 3" but is actually only 4' 9". A fiery Spanish woman, she was born in Guatemala, Central America under an extremely strict Catholic upbringing.

---

8   Carlos Castillo Armas, Wikipedia, http://en. wikipedia. org/wiki/Carlos_ Castillo_Armas

My father is 51 years old when I was born, much taller than my mother at 5' 5 1/2". He is bald in the middle with incredibly old, aging skin that makes him look older than his age. He is no longer the handsome man that courted my mother in 1940. He is a life-long smoker, smoking only unfiltered cigarettes like Camel or Lucky Strikes.

I hate the smell of cigarettes and wonder why my father likes smoking so much. He was born and raised Protestant in Cleveland, Ohio, and rarely ever attended church. He comes from an exceptionally large Irish/American family that settled in Cleveland from Ireland around 1850.

I never knew much about my father, as he never talked about his childhood. I always wondered why my father never learned to drive. Did he have girlfriends before my mother? What was it like growing up in that large Irish family in Cleveland?

Our family was raised on the lower west-side of Cleveland in a new development for low-income earners known as the housing project. We were forced into this awful crime ridden place when my father's family business burned down, and he had no insurance. Since he had no skills, he settled for work as a night watchman for minimum wage. My mother was not allowed to work, so money was always an issue for our family.

I'm very angry at both my parents for not being better educated and not having the drive to do better financial. And why did my father not protect us by having insurance.

My mother and father argue about our upbringing, but she easily wins the argument that we will all be raised Catholic, not Protestant as my father wants. Going to Catholic school creates a range of problems for me.

As always, my mother with her dominant ways, gets her way and forces my father to accept her decision. I hate the way my mother favors my older brother over my younger brother and I. She treats him like he is a baby, while we are ignored.

During my elementary school days at St. Malachi's Catholic School, I am routinely picked on by several bullies that are several years older. They push me around the school yard during recess and make fun of my olive complexion because I am not white like them. This gives me a complex that I try to solve by scraping my face at night with sandpaper, but my skin still does not turn white.

But the worst thing they did was when I said my father was a hero in World War II, they laughed and said, "That old guy, he's older than my grandfather, maybe he was in the Revolutionary War." They keep laughing and I leave in tears.

I asked my father about his war experience and find out he was in World War I. From that point, I'm totally ashamed and embarrassed by him.

The bullying problem ended when my older brother Willy, beat the crap out of the bigger bully.

But my bigger problem is with several Catholic nuns. Some nuns would routinely yell and punish me for little things. One nun was so mean that she took away my Elvis Presley cards and said, "You shouldn't be looking at that trash." I never got them back and hated the Catholic nuns and my mother for putting me in this situation in which there was no escape.

In 1957, we move to a better neighborhood on the Westside of Cleveland. Soon, I became one of a group of six friends. We are all the same age, except Denny who is two years younger. Our group has that kind of strong friendship and bonding that rarely happens. I feel certain we will all remain lifelong friends. We come from different nationalities, but all of our families are very patriotic Americans.

Denny is Polish, tall and lanky at 6' 2", with blond hair, and movie star good looks like Robert Redford. His two older brothers served in the U. S. Army.

Billy, short at 5' 8", is a wild Irishman, with flaming red hair, a hot temper, and fear of no man. He reminds me of Jerry Lee Lewis in looks and mannerisms. Billy's stepfather served with the U. S. Marines during the Korean War.

Ray at 5' 9", has blond hair like his namesake Sicilian Italian family. He has the good looks and charm of Paul Newman. He is a great bowler and could easily turn pro. His father and his six uncles all served in the U. S. Army during World War II.

Geno, Ukrainian, 5' 11" with dark brown hair, rarely smiles and reminds me of James Dean. He is probably the best athlete of us all. His father served in the underground Ukrainian Army during World War II and engaged in a series of deadly guerrilla conflicts against Nazi Germany.

John, Slovenian, nearly 6 ft tall, and built like a linebacker, could be a double for a young John Wayne. He possesses a major league fastball that could be his ticket to the big leagues. His father and all seven uncles served in the Navy during World War II.

At 5' 6", I am the shortest of the guys. With my blue/black hair and Irish/Spanish combination, I have been compared to Al Pacino or George Chakiris. With my blazing foot speed and rocket throwing arm, I might have made it to the big leagues in baseball, if not for my bad eyesight. My father, a war hero in World War I, received the Silver Star and Purple Heart. He told me extraordinarily little about his war experience:

My father served with the 4th Infantry Division, 59th Infantry Regiment, Company K, during his enlistment from May 28, 1918, to August 12, 1919, in World War I. His main duty was that of "runner." This was an extremely dangerous job that required him to carry messages back and forth from the command staff to fighting units near the battlefield. He participated in the Meuse-Argonne Offensive in France, the largest and bloodiest operation in World War I. It was also the deadliest battle in American history, in which 26,277 Americans were killed. [9]

---

9   From my father's war records that I sent for.

Some of the relatives said he was "shell shocked", a term that I did not understand or what exactly was wrong with him:

Shell Shock was a term coined in 1917 by Medical Officer Charles Myers, to describe the type of posttraumatic stress many soldiers were afflicted with. It was also known as "war neurosis" and "combat stress." At first shell shock was thought to be caused by soldiers being exposed to exploding shells. [10].

My Catholic studies continued at Blessed Sacrament Grade School. I hate Catholic school and do as little as possible in the way of studying and get poor grades. Since you need good grades to move on to high school in a Catholic school, I guaranteed myself no chance to be admitted to a Catholic high school.

Of course, I would never tell me mother what I was thinking and doing. By the end of my fifth year, Sister Kathleen Gotham, has red-lined me as a C- student, dooming me to failure in life according to their grading system.

Because of our move, I must start school in the middle of my fifth grade. The transfer puts me way behind in my studies and I receive my final report card with a failing status. This meant I must repeat the fifth grade.

All summer long I fretted about how to tell my mother about my failure. I decided not to tell her. I pretended that nothing happened and finally summer comes to an end and the next term comes around. I walked into the sixth grade and hope for the best.

My new teacher is the ruthless and sadistic, Sister Viola de Paddle. She took the roll call of everyone in the room and all the names were called but mine. The sweat is running down my face as Sister Viola de Paddle stares at me. She asked me what my name is and then left for what seemed like hours. I felt that the game is up. But to my surprise, she returns and gives me a seat assignment. I made it to the sixth grade. Not bad for a lowly C- student.

---

10   Shell Shock - http://www. bbc. uk/insideout/extra/series-1/shell-shocked. shtml

Sister Viola de Paddle hated anyone that defied her rules. Evil and wicked people who disobeyed her were banished to the back of the room, away from the good and holy people. She especially hated me and would be little me constantly about what an evil and stupid boy I was.

One day my punishment was completely different. Sister Viola de Paddle said that instead of going to the back of the room, I was to report to Sister Gertrude Withered, the fourth-grade teacher. I wondered what my punishment would be. Would my legs be burned with a red-hot poker to exorcise the devil out of me? Or will she pull out one of my toenails with a rusty pair of tweezers.

When I got to the fourth grade, my punishment was far greater than anything I expected. Sister Gertrude Withered said that was to be my new home. I felt sick. How was I going to explain to my mother that in one day, I had lost two years of schooling? But then, Sister Gertrude Withered she said that all the chairs were filled and to go back to the sixth grade. I had to laugh at Sister because I saw many empty chairs.

In the eighth grade, I went to church to confess my sins of missing Sunday mass twice, a huge sacrilege that could doom me to hell. On that day, I had the misfortune of confessing to Father Jonathan de Costa Inclement.

As soon as the words fell out of my mouth, Father Inclement exploded in a violent rage about what a horrible sinner I was. As I left the "private booth", I was stared at by everyone in the filled church.

After that, my hatred of the Catholic church was complete. I wanted nothing to do with "these people" and would not attend church again. I did not think that priests and nuns following the solemn vow of chastity, was working very well for many of them.

One late night, during my fifteenth year on earth, I am awoken by a violent argument between my mother and father. He's SCREAMING at her, "You whore! What are you doing out so late with your Tony."

She says to him in a harsh tone, "Si, soy la puta de Tony. Viejo Mierda."

This sets my father into a rage. He slaps her across the face. She falls down but is quickly up on her feet YELLING, "I wan devorse. I wan you go out of house."

The next day, my father leaves the house, and my parents are getting a divorce.

I thought my mother had treated my father badly. She then burned all pictures of my father so we would never know what he looked like. She thought that would wipe his memory away but all it did for me was further increase my hatred of her.

Within a few weeks, the divorce is final, and Tony is living in our house. Months later, my mother and Tony are married. My new stepfather and I got along well, but my younger brother Rudy, hated him. I would only see my father on weekends, but he appeared to be happy in his new life.

I started the 9th grade at a public school, glad to be rid of the Catholic nuns. This was the first year West Technical High School had added a 9th grade. With the addition of a 9th grade, our high school, with a student body of 4,000, is now the largest high school in the state of Ohio.

The size of the student body has some pluses and minuses for me. Since I am very shy and not one of the cool people, I can blend in and not be noticed. To be in with the cool people, you either had to be able to dance (which I did not) or play some sport (which I did not). Because of my shyness, I had never been on a date.

The closest I came to a date was when a cute girl on the school bus I knew invited me to come over on Friday so she would make a Spaghetti dinner for us. I was terrified and did not know how to respond, so I just smiled and walked past her.

To try and get in with the cool people, my clearest path would be to get on the football team. Since I was a good athlete, I was certain I could make the team. But not having a car, any money, or not being able to land a part-time job, forced me to abandon my dream. The five mile walk each way doomed me to be a "nobody", never to go on dates, never have a girlfriend, and never be able to attend my senior prom.

Since West Tech is a well-regarded technical trade school, I would have an opportunity to learn a trade and get a good-paying blue-collar job when I graduated. I decided to become an Auto Mechanic and envisioned many women linings up to date me. But my hopes were soon dashed when I found out that what I thought was an entry level class, is really a class for guys with lots of automotive experience.

I struggled mightily to try and keep up and might have done well, except for that awful day when I messed up a simple oil and filter change job. After changing everything and adding new oil, I forgot to tighten the oil plug enough. When the teacher drove the car away, oil leaked all over his new classroom floor. He exploded in a rage at me, "You idiot. Look what you have done. You clean this floor up now. I do not want you touching another car again. From now on you will only sweep the floors and I will pass you with a D."

Because I did so poorly in grade school, I struggled with most of my classes and failed three courses. I had to attend summer school to graduate in August of 1965. My 1. 99/4. 00 grade point average was good enough to graduate at the bottom of my class. I was not sure I would be able to get any job, but my stepfather Tony had connections at the Ford Motor Company and within a month, I had a great paying job at Ford making $2. 67/hour.

From August 1965 till August 1966, my five best friends and I went to parties, drank beer, dated women, bowled, and played sports. Despite all of this, Vietnam was always in the back of our minds. Many nights we talked about the service and reviewed our options. Many men were dodging the draft, some were burning their draft cards, but none from our group thought to escape military service via a student deferment, getting married, or running away to Canada.

On June 1966 I received a letter from Uncle Sam, with the familiar "Greetings" letting me know that I was being drafted. My buddy Geno got his letter about the same time. Geno and I had talked about joining the Marines under the buddy plan, but I opted for the Army because it was only a two-year commitment vs. the three years for the Marines.

Denny, who was only 17, begged his parents to let him join the Army and they agreed. Denny and I left together on August 10, 1966. Geno volunteered for the Marines and left shortly after Denny and I. Billy who had a deferment because he had lost his spleen in a car accident many years ago, did not have to go in the service, but was determined to join us and volunteered for the Army and would leave in a few months.

Ray and John quickly joined the Navy under the Navy Buddy Enlistment program with an enlistment contract of four years. They would leave in February 1967 for the Great Lakes Boot camp on the shores of Lake Michigan.

The buddy plan provided for up to four individuals who wanted to remain together, if possible, during their enlistment.

Three days before we were to leave, Geno's father threw a huge party for us at his house. News of the party quickly got around and there were over one hundred at the party. Many beautiful young women wanted to see us off and I was hoping that someone I wanted to see again would be there. And there she was, Wild Thing.

Annie G. is sixteen with beautiful shoulder-length lustrous brown hair. She had the face of an angel on a very shapely figure. Her beautiful white teeth showed as she smiled at me. I first met Annie a few months ago at a church festival. She had asked my younger brother Rudy whether I was dating anyone. I stopped to talk with Annie. I loved her unique personality, confidence, and outgoing manner. That is when I first called her Wild Thing.

She laughed and said, "Why are you calling me Wild Thing?" I said, "I've named you after this year's big hit by The Troggs called Wild Thing. You fit the song words perfectly."

We hit it off very well that night as we talked, laughed, and got to know each other better. When the night was coming to an end, Annie said, "Do you want to do something wild?"

I am thinking lucky me till she points to a garage and says, "Let's climb up on that garage.", so we did.

Later, the garage, she kissed me goodbye. I said, "I'm leaving for the Army in two days. I hope to see you again." She said nothing as we climbed down. As Annie started to leave, she hugged me and said, "We'll see." and she left.

The next day, as I was preparing to leave, Annie's younger sister gave me a note from Annie. In the note Annie said that she wanted to write me while I was away, and she enclosed her address.

My normal life has now become overly complicated. I have never fired a weapon, do not like violence, and have this awful feeling that something bad is going to happen to me if I go to Vietnam. I expect to be severely injured or killed.

On August 10, 1966, Denny and I, and a few other hundred draftees, board a train in Cleveland for a three-day trip to Fort Benning. The big highlight of the trip was when some truck tried to run a train stop. Our train tried to stop but could not. The truck is dragged about a quarter of a mile and split in two. On the train we never knew what happened until the train stopped and they told us.

"Is this an omen of things to come?"

Soon as we got off the train, we are treated to Georgia's legendary humidity and temperatures in the high 90s. We are taken by bus to Fort Benning, a huge United States Army base that straddles the Alabama-Georgia border next to Columbus, Georgia. It's mission, to "produce the world's finest combat infantrymen." Fort Benning was to be my home away from home for the next eight weeks.

As we got off the bus, we are greeted by some madman called a Drill Sergeant. He is yelling orders nonstop. Someone had made a stupid remark and soon was talking to a tree saying, "I'm sorry drill sergeant", over and over. Other minor offenses were greeted with, "Drop down and give me fifty pushups", which few were able to do, and they were mocked mercilessly. The next day, all our hair is cut off to allow the Georgian sun to burn our heads. Later that day, I had my first southern meal and found the food tasteless. Some of my "Southern friends" still thought the Civil War was going on and called those of us from the north, "Yankees."

For the next eight weeks, I was subject to a grueling, anxiety-provoking program called "basic training." The basic idea was to break your mind and body and then mold you into a fighting soldier that "never questions why, but to do or die."During this long day, Drill Sergeants yelled at you for anything you did wrong.

After eight weeks of basic training, you are usually allowed to go home for about a month before starting your next assignment. I was looking forward to going home for a thirty-day leave before moving on to advanced training. Unfortunately for me, there would be no thirty-day break after basic training. The need for more soldiers in Vietnam overruled us getting a break. Too many guys were being killed in Vietnam and replacements were needed badly. All leaves were cancelled immediately. The announcement was made that about ninety-five percent of us would become infantrymen.

To begin, the conditioning of the body, the mind, and the spirit, needed to become an infantryman required specialized training. No place was better suited to give us this type of training than Fort Polk. The fort, located ten miles east of Leesville, Louisiana, is best known as "Tigerland". Louisiana's heat, muggy conditions, and precipitation closely mimicked the environmental conditions of South Vietnam. Therefore, it provided an ideal location for infantry training about the jungles of Vietnam.

You knew you were being trained for Infantry the minute the buses pulled up to the gates of "Tigerland". As you enter the huge complex, you see this exceptionally large billboard with Tigers in a jungle setting with the words, "Welcome to Tigerland. Every man a Tiger, "RRAHHH."

60,000-70,000 men a year were trained in Infantry tactics to prepare for Vietnam.

Coming into Tigerland, we see row after row of old wooden two- and three-story buildings that numbered into the thousands. These buildings, built in 1941, made of wood, are huge fire hazards that are guarded twenty-four hours a day by us, the newly recruited "visitors." On the buildings are the emblems of elite Infantry patches and various emblems for medals of valor. Returning war heroes from Vietnam were our drill sergeants and instructors.

Company after company of infantrymen, thousands upon thousands of soldiers marched in perfect formation to the musical tones of a drill sergeants' cadence,

"I want to be an Airborne Ranger"

"I want to live a life of danger"

"Airborne! Airborne! All the Way!"

It is a beautiful sight to see and hear. One of those drill sergeants leading the chants, was Platoon Sergeant George Smith. He is a proud Army lifer of over twenty years. Old for the Army at 45 years of age, his distinct sounds can be heard for miles. He has an unusual tone that is high pitched, almost feminine.

Our day starts promptly at 4:30 a. m. as we are awakened by drill sergeants, flipping on bright lights in the barracks, roaming and blowing whistles at the top of their lungs. Those who don't respond to this delightful wake-up call are rudely flipped out of their mattresses.

At 5am, dressed in full combat gear, company after company would run in formation for two miles chanting the familiar airborne chant. Breakfast followed at 5:30 a. m. Two hundred men companies enter and exit the mess hall in ten minutes max. We sat down, ate very quickly, never looking to our front or looking up. Our heads were down and eating. Talking was strictly forbidden, as were seconds.

The conditioning resumed after breakfast with constant formations being called every 10-15 minutes. These formations were designed to build reaction and response time to simulate battlefield conditions. Every hour or so, whistles were blowing for us to "move out" and get into formations. This would go on day after day for several weeks. Then it suddenly ended. We had passed the test and were ready.

Our instructors told us about some of the tactics and weapons that the Vietcong used against us: Bouncing Betty mines that you never saw that were triggered by the release of pressure on the arming mechanism. If you stepped on the Bouncing Betty and released your weight, it would explode at chest height. The punji pits were holes dug in the ground with sharp spears pointing straight up and covered with leaves so you would step on and fall into the pit.

A small portion of Fort Polk is filled with dense, jungle-like vegetation, that somewhat duplicated the terrain and conditions to be found in the jungles of Vietnam. The last three days were spent in "the jungle", called the Vietnam Village, a miniature Vietcong base camp complete with various huts made of straw.

It was designed to expose you to what the villages looked like in Vietnam, various booby traps, night ambushes in the chilling rain and pitch darkness, and being on guard duty all night long with little sleep.

We camped on the outside in an open field, facing the woods. Around 3 a. m. , we would be attacked by fake VC who would fire at us with blank rounds. They would try and sneak in, take our weapons, slit our throats with red paint, and then crawl away and start shooting. Trainees who sleep through the night, woke up to find their weapons missing and throats slit with red paint.

The most interesting part of our jungle training was called "Survival Week". The first two days we were paired into groups of four and given a compass, a map, and a few days of food. Our job was to arrive at a series of check points without being captured. It was a very cold and rainy and it would be easy to give up, but what kept us going was the daily reminders by our drill sergeants that we were going to Vietnam and that very few of us would return alive.

At the end of our training, we were assembled in outside bleachers to hear a chilling speech as to why we are going to Vietnam and why

Vietnam is so vital to American security. Using a chalk board as he talked, the 1st Sergeant delivered the famous theory called "the domino effect", first publicized by President Dwight Eisenhower in 1954. In this theory, Russia and China were trying to take over countries one by one, starting with Vietnam, until they had total control of Asia. If this worked, they would keep on taking countries unchallenged.

After eight weeks, we were given orders for our next assignment. As expected, my orders read to report to Oakland, California at 0800 hours on January 3, 1967, to be processed for Infantry duty in Vietnam. Since I didn't get my required thirty days leave after basic training, I was on my way home for a required 30-day leave before my trip to Vietnam.

I was afraid to leave my home, not knowing when or if, I might die. That was almost as fearful as actually dying.

Of the 3,000,00 who served in Vietnam, about 300,000 were in combat positions. Of these, approximately 30,000 were killed. Therefore, your odds of dying was about one in ten. [11]

---

11   Statistics about the Vietnam War, www. vhfcn. org/stat. hrml

CHAPTER 3

Welcome to South Vietnam

(January 1967)

My thirty days leave at home is not the joyous occasion that I had envisioned. All the guys, except Billy are home for the holidays. Ray and John leave for stateside duty in a about a month. Geno, Denny, and Billy are all headed to Vietnam.

My mother is worried sick about me leaving and thinks I'm going to die. She has gotten me a rosary, blessed by the Pope, that I promise to wear daily while in Vietnam. And my father, who has been healthy all his life, is admitted to the hospital with some kind of respiratory disease.

My two brothers and I arrived at the hospital to find my father sleeping in his bed. He has an oxygen mask over his mouth and nose. He's thinner, maybe ten pounds or more, then when I saw him last in June. There are huge dark circles under his sleepy eyes that were not there before. His face, so thin, almost skeleton like, that I barely recognize the man I've known as "Papa" for so long.

The doctor meets with us to discuss my father's condition. Dr. Johnson begins, "Your father is suffering from emphysema, a progressive disease of the lungs that primarily causes shortness of breath."

"This disease is a slow, painful, exhausting death that takes many years before death occurs. He will have to wear oxygen to survive and will never breathe as before. I'm sorry to say that his last days will be filled with depression, anxiety, irregular breathing, and cool extremities'. He may lose his sense of direction and experience discoloring of his skin. His wheezing will get much worse, sounding like a cat whining, that becomes louder and louder."

I ask, "How long do you think he has to live?"

Dr. Johnson responds, "It's hard to say, 3-5 years is possible, maybe longer. We will release him within a few days so he can return to his apartment. He will provide him with a portable oxygen tank and some maintenance medicines."

On January 3, 1967, I was on a plane from Cleveland to Oakland to begin my long journey. Three days later, we left for Travis Air Force Base, just outside of Oakland, for the 13,000-mile, forty-hour trip to South Vietnam. Our first stop was the Wake Islands for a fuel stop and within a few hours we were to be bound for Vietnam, but our airplane developed some kind of mechanical problem forcing an emergency landing at Clark Air Base in the Philippine Islands. For three wonderful days we were "stranded" on this beautiful island with green lush scenic landscape and perfect weather.

The first day we were taken to some large outdoor training area and sat in bleachers to hear a seminar on becoming a dog trainer. We would train for about six months on the island with a German Shepherd and then spend the last six months of our tour in Vietnam as a dog handler. I passed on the opportunity. However, many of the soldiers were eager to volunteer.

Two days later, we were in the air again and landed at Tan Son Nhut Airport in Saigon, Vietnam. It was early afternoon as we walked down the steps of the aircraft and were greeted by temperatures in the 90's. The blast of heat almost knocked me over. I was grasping for a breath of air. Now I know what it must be like to be food cooking inside of an oven.

Green lush trees, by the hundreds, lay a few thousand feet to my right and left. It seemed impossible that we were in a war zone. It felt more like being on a tropical island getting ready to start a vacation. Within a few minutes, the reality of war came into view as several Army 1/4-ton trucks are heading our way. They held seating for about twenty. The unusual thing about the trucks was that they were heavily armed and were enclosed with steel bars across the top and sides. The driver said the bars were to protect us from VC throwing grenades inside the trucks.

Our trucks were escorted by two large tanks as we traveled from Bien Hoa, the largest US base outside of the continental United States, to the 90th Replacement Center in Long Binh. This is the first stop for newly arriving replacements that would be sent to various units within South Vietnam. It is also the final stop before you leave Vietnam.

As we proceeded through Saigon, I thought what a contrast this city was to my hometown of Cleveland, Ohio. The buildings are old and heavily influenced by French architecture. There are few automobiles. Most of the people are wearing funny straw hats, riding bicycles or some strange form of transportation resembling automobiles from the early 1920's.

As we pulled out of the bustling city of Saigon, the atmosphere changes drastically. The city gives way to villages that contained row upon row of one-story huts made of straw, wood, and some form of cardboard or aluminum strips as its roof. The huts are very small, probably no more than 200 square feet, smaller than the size of a basic American living room. There are no grocery stores, restaurants, fast food places, shopping malls, banks, fire departments, or police stations. Out of nowhere we come upon a multi-million-dollar Exxon gas station, used to resupply American vehicles. It seemed out of place in this poor country.

An hour later, we arrived at the 90th Replacement Center in Long Binh. While our stay was a short three days, we learned much about popular sayings and goings on in Vietnam.

The first thing you hear about is the very important DEROS date, the date you leave Vietnam for the states. Signs of "DEROS" are on the faces of veterans who had completed their tours. They are about my age, but their faces and mannerisms are of a much older person. They rarely smiled and look tough as nails with deep suntans. They are called "short-timers". You are "short" when your tour of duty is almost complete. You know instantly who they are by the wooden canes they carried. The shorter the cane, the shorter the time remaining in country. They let you know how short they are by shouting out, "Short - 3 days", some as low as "1 hour."

The rotation policy on your tour was for one year, but about every three months the "short-timers" would leave and the "new guys", like me, would arrive to replace them. This was done so that a mix of old and new soldiers were always out in the field. The Army had established our in-country tour length at 12 months. Only small numbers of soldiers would volunteer for multiple tours in Vietnam.

They called us "FNG" or "Fuckin New Guys", who were feared and not trusted because we knew almost nothing and could get an experienced soldier killed. REMF's, or "Rear Echelon Mother Fucker's", were the support troops in the safest parts of Vietnam who saw no combat and had the comforts of home that combat soldiers would never have. They had swimming pools, restaurants, bowling alleys, golf courses, hot showers, and even an ice cream stand.

If you get three Purple Hearts, you don't have to out into the jungle anymore. There were stories of soldiers who feared combat so much, they took their M-16 rifle and blew their knee cap off. They figured it was a small sacrifice to walk with a limp for life to escape the field and be sent home alive.

On day three, my orders came down that I was assigned to the famed First Infantry Division, also called the "Big Red One." The next day we are taken by truck to DiAn ("Zee-on"), about 20 km outside of Saigon. This is the in-processing unit of the First Infantry Division. As we entered the center, we saw a huge billboard with the 1st Infantry Division Motto:

"No Mission too difficult, No Sacrifice too great. Duty First."

After a few days of processing, we are taken to an area close to our permanent location. It is a large tent in the middle of nowhere. The dark and eerie location made you feel unsafe. Late at night, we were hit with mortars. This was my first encounter with the enemy. I'm trembling uncontrollably. My hands are shaking. For the first time in Vietnam, I'm terrified. I don't feel very safe. I'm thinking, "I don't want to be here. I want to go home now."

The next morning, I was on my way to my permanent location called "LaiKhe" (Lie-Kay). I was being assigned to the 2nd Battalion of the 28th Infantry Regiment, Charlie company, one of three rifle companies at LaiKhe. The other two companies are Alpha and Bravo companies.

Laikhe, a village in an abandoned rubber plantation, is about thirty miles north of Saigon. Sandbags are placed throughout the company area to protect us from incoming mortar fire. The 1st Infantry Division picked LaiKhe as a base camp because of its strategic location on the Ho Chi Minh Trial, a direct line between Cambodia and Saigon.

Inside LaiKhe, are dozens of old French colonial homes and a large swimming pool that was built by the French. The pool is run by the U. S. Army. The Vietnamese village sells products and services like the steam room, where for $2 you could get a steam bath.

However, the biggest draw was the bar where "numbered girls" were made available to us for two Saigon teas (Saigon tea was basically colored water or soda) and five dollars. Girls who wore numbers were deemed "safe", since they were checked by our doctors. "The Crossroads", located in the middle of LaiKhe, has a barber shop and other local shops run by the Vietnamese.

Around the village is fencing and barbed wire and is patrolled nightly by the Military Police (MPs). There is a nighttime curfew for the entire village. LaiKhe is very safe except for constant mortar and rocket attacks, earning it the nickname "Rocket City." I thought our own Highway 13 was safe, but found it was nicknamed "Thunder Road" since LaiKhe was positioned to stop the enemy from entering Saigon via the Ho Chi Minh Trail.

When I arrive at Charlie company, I get my first glimpse of Vietnamese women and find them to be extremely unattractive. When they smile, you see rows of ugly black stained teeth with many missing teeth. "Betel Nut", was used to relieve the pain of diseased gums, but the long-term affect was to blacken the few teeth they had.

The typical Vietnamese male is around 5' 1" to 5' 2" inches in height and weight around 120 pounds. The Vietnamese language produced irritating high-pitched squeaky sounds.

The next day, we received five days of jungle training that is required for all FNG's. During the first three days, we learned about the enemy and some of their tactics.

The last two days of training was about the tactics we would use to fight the Viet Cong:

The main tactic we will be involved with, Search and Destroy, is a military strategy used to slow down and kill Viet Cong in a hostile area, usually jungles. We will be inserted in the jungles, search for the enemy, destroy the enemy, and then withdraw back to our base camps.

During these missions, we will patrol the jungles with a 35-pound load that starts with a harness that goes over the shoulders secured around the waist. Attached to that harness, is one large compress bandage, one to two smoke grenades and several small sacks for carrying 2-3 hand grenades, or for carrying ammo if carrying the M-16 rifle. Some preferred to carry the magazines, for the M-16 in cloth bandoliers draped across their chest in a crossing pattern.

Everyone gets the standard issue plastic jungle canteens filled with cold water that quickly becomes warm water. The water is attached to our harness. The standard issue is two canteens and each canteen held about a quart of water. It is a heavy load, but necessary because of the heat and humidity.

At the beginning of a mission, we add around sixty more pounds to our normal thirty-five pounds. This load will help us to survive at least three days in the field with enough food and essentials if cut-off from any help.

The extra sixty pounds starts with a lightweight rucksack that is filled and kept repacking until it is comfortable. We will have three pairs of socks, foot powder, a green plastic poncho with a quilted liner blanket, a must for cold nights or on ambush patrols to keep the mosquitoes from biting you all night. The plastic poncho will serve double duty. It keeps us dry from the rain and also used as part of a two-man tent. To that tent, we add our rubber mattress, to keep us off of the water when it rains. It also provided a very comfortable sleep. Everyone is required to carry a claymore mine and an entrenching tool for digging.

We are required to wear two dog tags around our neck. If we were killed, it will help to ID us. I taped them together to cut the down the noise they make while walking in the jungle. Also attached to my dog tags is my P-38 can opener.

Most infantrymen carry the M-16 rifle, weighing around eight pounds, with twelve to twenty magazines of ammo that weighed from eight pounds to fourteen pounds. The magazine can hold twenty rounds, but we never loaded it with more than eighteen rounds, or it will jam. Leaving out two rounds puts less stress on the spring. A shorter version of the M-16 rifles, called the CAR-15, is available, but mostly given to officers and a select few.

The weapon I carried was the M-79 Grenade launcher. It was a breach open, single shot weapon that fired a 40MM grenade cartridge. It is accurate up to 300 meters. It is a very reliable weapon. However, the round had to go around seven meters and hit something before it would explode. This was not the best weapon to have in a jungle where you don't get seven meters of open space. There were shotgun type shells, called canister rounds, that solved the problem, but they were hard to obtain. The M-79 weighed around six pounds, but a typical load of 25 rounds was very heavy since each round weighed ten ounces each.

After five days of jungle training, we were given our jungle uniforms. Everything had to be green. There were green socks with green underwear boxer shorts. The standard fatigue jacket and trousers are lightweight and in green. We could add items to our jungle jacket such as our name, rank, unit patch, and a Combat Infantry Badge (CIB). Items on our jungle jacket had to be in black to blend in and not attract attention in the jungle. The jungle boots are very comfortable and lightweight with drain holes to let water out making them quick drying.

The next day, I went out with my squad of ten on my very first ambush patrol just outside of LaiKhe. The purpose of ambush patrols is to go out a few thousand meters away from the company area, setup all night and give early warning to the rest of the company if we detected any enemy that might be approaching. I found it very scary to be in the middle of nowhere with only ten men and no help if things went bad. That night, I stayed up all night listening for possible enemy movements. It didn't seem to bother the experienced guys much as they slept through much of the night. I didn't realize that this was a pretty safe area.

On my way back to the company area, I hear our platoon Sergeant Johnson, yell over at me, "Hey Kurparick, y'all comon overhear."

One of the other guys, David Laub from Ohio, had told me about Johnson. "He's a no-nonsense, tough-as-nails Army lifer. He takes no shit from anyone. A few days ago, your squad leader said something stupid, and Johnson slapped him across the face." I'm wondering what I have done wrong as I head towards Sergeant Johnson.

Johnson says that name is too long. I'm gonna call you Kirk from now on. Where y'all kinfolk from Kirk?" I'm from Ohio Sergeant Johnson." He responds back, "Aah recon y'all was a yankee. Y'all can call me Willie C. I'm from Savannah, near Adlanna. My wife Barbara is the purtiest gal in the South and I'm fixin to see her quick like again. But y'all squad leader ain't got but fowar brann cells in his head and I done had it with him. So I'm fixin to take y'all under my wing so we can all can get home. You best not open your mouth and listen here. You stay away from this old heifer woman here and their diseases."

I said, thank you Willie C, I'll be listening to everything you teach me. Have you been in the Army long?" Willie C says, "I'm twenty-six now and I got fared from my job after hi-school and got this here oppahtunity to join the Army. Ahda gonda college if adha bin smaretore."

I'm very grateful and blessed that Sergeant Johnson has taken me under his wing. I'm feeling better about my chances of surviving Vietnam. I hope to visit Willie C. in Atlanta and meet his beloved Barbara.

CHAPTER 4

A Slaughter is Coming

(January 1967 - October16, 1967)

Our daily patrols are called Search and Destroy Missions. [12] Usually, we are involved in one Search and Destroy mission per month that could last for periods of up to three weeks. Some missions are more dangerous than others.

During my one-year tour, from January 1967 to January 1968, the First Infantry participated in ten combat operations. The First Infantry also participated in two major battles in 1967 that produced two completely different results. I was involved in all ten of those operations. For this, I was awarded the Air Medal, a rare decoration for an infantryman.

The Air Medal was awarded to anyone who, while serving in or with the Armed Forces of the United States, flew in twenty-five hours of combat assaults, during which exposure to enemy fire is probable and expected.

All missions start with trucks that take us to the airstrip at LaiKhe. Waiting at the airstrip, is the 173rd Assault Helicopter Company, with row upon rows of Huey UH-1 helicopters. The long blade of

---

12   Search and Destroy Missions - Annual 2nd Battalion 28th Infantry History, Black Lions, Republic of Vietnam, 1967

the helicopter would rotate slowly, then faster and faster till the blade is almost invisible. The sounds of the motors and propellers going produce the distinctive **"Whomp-Whomp"** sound that can be heard for miles and makes verbal communication difficult.

In the air, we have a beautiful view of the rich farmland, rice paddies, and row after row of trees that formed the jungle. The Huey's moved in a line like giant locusts. As they get closer to our landing area (LZ), the choppers would get into a staggered formation.

The placing of troops on the ground was called an air assault, a critical time for a helicopter, as a descending chopper is an easy target. You have to unload quickly or be kicked off, so no doors are on choppers. If the ground was muddy, the choppers would not land completely. They would hover a few feet above the ground. Getting off the chopper always sent chills down my spine and a tightening in my stomach.

After unloading, we moved to a predetermined site where we would set up camp. In military terms, this was called the Night Defensive Position (NDP). At the NDP, we were in a circle. In our assigned spots, we would dig foxholes first and then setup our two-man tents. At night, we would put out our trip flares and Claymore mines.

A foxhole is a type of defensive strategic position. Basically, it is a hole in the ground that you dig with a shovel. Typically, it is shoulder deep, three feet wide, and five feet long that holds two soldiers who can stand and fire a weapon. To the front and sides, you add sandbags filled with dirt and cover the top with support logs across the top and then add sandbags on top.

Trip flares are triggered if someone inadvertently pulls a concealed wire. This sets off the flare that would burn with a bright light and illuminate the area.

The Claymore mine, shaped like a car's brake shoe, is made to sit above the surface on a pair of tiny metal tripods. Since it was a directional mine, it was very important to make sure the side "Front Towards Enemy", is pointing that way before inserting the blasting cap.

At night we used touch to place them in the right direction using the curved shape. Unfortunately, so did the VC. They would try to turn the Claymore to face towards us. When a Claymore mine is set off, it unleashed several hundred tiny steel balls in a sixty-degree arc with a deadly range of fifty meters.

We setup Listening Posts (LP's), fifty meters outside of the NDP, to give early warning of approaching VC. There were usually two men to each LP. They went all around the NDP.

For further protection, one squad (about ten men), from each company, would go out about 500 to 1000 meters from the NDP and setup an ambush site. I found these ambush events to be very dangerous and stressful while in Vietnam.

At night, I wore my boots and held my weapon across my chest as I tried to sleep.

Usually, we stayed out in the field for about three weeks. During that time, we lived like animals. We rarely, if ever, took a bath or a shower. We didn't use deodorants. We lived in the same boots and uniforms for those three weeks.

After weeks of patrolling the jungles in never ending rain and heat, or dust and heat, our uniforms and boots would start to fall apart. Our black boots would get caked on with dust and dirt. Our boots bleached white from scuffs, dust, and the sun and the soles are nearly gone.

Many uniforms would get ripped or torn traveling through the jungle. The constant dampness would rot the seams and weaken the threads. If we had to stay longer than three weeks, we would get new uniforms and sometimes even new boots. After our mission was complete, Choppers would come back and "extract" us out at the LZ and take us back to LaiKhe.

Operation Cedar Falls - January 9 to January 17, 1967. The area was called the "Iron Triangle" because it was very similar to an area in the Korean peninsula that was also called the "Iron Triangle" during the Korean War. The area is heavily fortified, and contains the VC Central Office of South Vietnam, known as COSVN. Their base camps and supply installations are laced by extensive, well-constructed underground bunkers and tunnel complexes. The area is known to be heavily mined, and booby trapped.

On the first day around noon, my company stopped in the jungle to have a tasty lunch of C-rations and Lukewarm water. A few minutes later, we hear an extremely loud explosion. One of the guys is leaning against a tree, and the pin from his grenade gets caught on a jungle vine and he pulls the pin accidently. This instantly kills him. Pieces of his body are thrown everywhere.

Later that day, being so tired from the heat and humidity, I keep falling and stumbling as I walk. I stumble again and bounce off a wire that was placed as a booby trap. In that instant, I'm thinking, I'm going to die. I wait for the explosion as I quickly move away from the trip-wire booby trap. No explosion. The grenade didn't go off. I'm scared to death as my heart is racing.

Operation Tucson - February 14 to February 17, 1967. The operation is in the area of a thirty-two-hundred-foot mountain, called Nui Ba Dinh by the Vietnamese. This mountain of dark black is a solitary peak on a flat plane, nicknamed "The Black Virgin Mountain" by U. S. troops.

On the first night, I was given a Starlight Scope with instructions to observe any movement. The Starlight Scope is used to see objects at night in green images. After looking through the scope for nearly an hour at night, I thought I saw movement.

I kept looking and saw what I believed was row after row of VC coming at us in a human wave. I was ready to start shooting my M-79 and run back to warn everyone. However, the more I looked, those "VCs" were not moving. I continued to look. Soon I realized I was looking at row after row of chopped down tree stumps.

No wonder FNG's are not to be trusted

The next day at LaiKhe, our company has a big award ceremony. Along with quite a few others, I'm awarded the CIB, short for **Combat Infantry Badge**. The CIB is a very elite badge that infantrymen cherish and one of the most prized of Army awards. To earn the CIB, you have to be in country for over one month and come under fire in a combat situation.

Operation Yorktown - March 18 to April 19, 1967. We try to be quiet as possible, walking through the jungles. However, there were always a few that were talking. A few might even light a cigarette, or someone with a death wish, might wear a white towel around their neck. The larger the group, the harder it was to move quietly.

That's why I wanted to be in front of everyone leading our company though the jungles. I felt much safer since I could control my own destiny. On this mission, I traded my M-79 for a M-16 rifle since I would get my chance to be a point man. The next day, I'm walking point for the company on a search and destroy mission.

A point man is the lead man advancing through hostile or unsecured territory in a company formation. He has to watch for snipers, booby traps, ambushes, and enemy movement. Being at the very front is one the most exposed and dangerous thing you can do. Walking point can be an extremely dangerous job. If you walk into an ambush, step on a mine, or trip a booby trap, you are likely to be the first one killed.

I walked along and my eyes are drawn immediately to a trail. My mind races back to Infantry training and the grim warnings from other Vietnam Veterans:

Never walk on trails.

If you have ever hiked, you have walked on a path. A path is narrow so that usually only one person can walk on it. It is natural, caused by humans and animals walking on. A trail is wider than a path and has the look and feel that someone could be living in that area. This is a HUGE DANGER sign that the enemy could be nearby.

I walked further along, staying off the trail. Then, the trail seems to disappear without warning. This seems very odd to me. I stop and turn around quickly to halt those behind me. I'm talking to my squad leader and he's now on the radio talking to the company commander. They decided, I will walk further along while the others keep a very safe distance.

I walked a few more feet and all heck broke loose. *Crack! Crack! Ping! Pop-pop-pop-pop!* I'm getting fire from a carbine rifle and other automatic weapons. Bullets are everywhere.

The life expectancy of a point man in a firefight is only seven seconds. I have to survive for at least seven seconds.

One thousand one. One thousand 2. One thousand 3.

Three VC have popped out from the ground from nowhere and are trying to kill me. I'm running, dodging, and zigzagging on a full gallop avoiding the bullets that seem to follow my every step.

One thousand four. One thousand five.

The bullets are hitting the ground around me. Dirt is flying everywhere.

One thousand six. One thousand seven.

I've survived for at least seven seconds, see an ant hill, and jump behind it. Within seconds, I yell, "Grenade", pull the pin and throw a grenade at the three VC and return fire. The firing has now stopped. I think I've killed them.

Later on, I'm sitting and leaning against a tree. I'm trembling uncontrollably and can't stop. My heart is beating so fast that I think it's going to explode. My hands are shaking. I wasn't scared while I was being shot at, but now it's different. Some officer is talking to my squad about their account of what happened. I heard that my squad leader, got a Bronze Star with "V", the machine gunner a Army Commendation with a "V" and maybe several others got medals.

An hour later, my platoon leader tells me to move out. I tell him, "I don't want to walk point." He says, "Why Not, just get moving." I didn't say anything and moved out.

As I'm walking, I can smell the odor of dead bodies. It's like the smell I remember back in Cleveland when they would slaughter cows at the slaughterhouses on the west side of Cleveland.

I didn't see anything till I move up a little further. I freeze. There is a pile of dead bodies. I'm trembling again. The others behind me have caught up. I'm pointing to the bodies, "Holy Shit look at that." The guy behind me says, "Look at what, I don't see anything." There was nothing there, my mind was playing tricks on me.

After walking point for another five hundred meters, I'm back to my normal self. The vegetation has become unusually thick but that didn't stop me from catching something that didn't look right. I see several short leafy tree leaves that are dead and brown. A big warning sign that made that area stand out.

I immediately had our platoon stop. We check the area and find a huge booby trap. A trip wire ran off the ground and was attached to two 60-mm mortar shells. The other end was attached to a tree at about head height. Both shells were rigged to go off together. The blast could have easily killed several from our platoon. Our platoon destroys the booby trap and we continued on our mission.

On April 16, my 3rd platoon, was out on a search and destroy mission with my squad in the lead. Glenn H. , on point, is walking on a trail. Kate, with the M-79, follows closely behind. A distant 3rd in the formation is Battles. I am closely behind Battles.

Within seconds, we hear a very loud explosion. A large Chinese mine has just exploded. The blast shreds Glenn and Kate, badly injuring both of them. The impact is so great that it knocks Battles off his feet, and he rolls into me, knocking me off my feet. Cries go out immediately. **Medic! Medic!** We are pinned down.

Medics are helping the badly injured Glenn and Kate. There is fire everywhere. Our platoon is engaged in a fierce firefight with a heavily entrenched and fortified VC platoon. 1st platoon is on the way to help us.

Our machine gunner, Willie Willis, is firing his machine gun on fully automatic. He is firing huge bursts of rounds without letting up on the trigger. I'm watching the barrel glow red-hot. It freezes up. The machine gun crew is working to pull the melted barrel off and replace it with another. Willis is hit.

All of us are getting fired upon and are pinned down. My heart is pounding. Sweat is rolling down my underarms. I'm sweating as if I'm in a sauna. I can feel the hairs on my head growing. Several of the guys near me are wounded. They are in the killing zone.

A killing zone is an area that is entirely covered by enemy fire. Soldiers within this zone are isolated and trapped.

Lt. Murphy has us run into the killing zone to pull the wounded out. We come under withering fire as we pull the wounded out. We run into the fire several times to get the wounded out to the LZ area.

As we are taking Willis out, I see a small hole on his stomach, and I think he will be ok. But they tell me he is dead. He has a huge hole on the other side of his back. I didn't know that Willis was bleeding to death. We continue to get the wounded out to the LZ, waiting for Medevac choppers to get them to hospitals. During the firefight, most of our weapon's jam and we toss them into a pile.

In the LZ area, I see a tall soldier from 1st platoon moving towards me. He is in complete distress. He can't talk. He's having trouble breathing. It looks like a bullet has hit his jaw. He writes the word "spoon" in the soft mud in front of me.

I happen to have a plastic spoon sticking in the front of my jacket. I use it to clear globs of giant clots of blood from his mouth. He seems to be breathing much better now. He then makes a circle motion around his head and face.

I wrap his jaw. I have to get on my tippy toes to wrap his wound. He is about six feet tall and much taller than me. He heads off towards the LZ and waiting choppers.

A total of six have been shot from Charlie company. Willis is the only one killed. This shakes me up since Willis is the first American soldier, I have seen that was killed. Our platoon leader, Lt. Billy Murphy is badly shaken by Willis's death. He is crying in pain.

Back at LaiKhe, Willie C says he wants me to take two new guys under my wing.

"Hey Kirk, we just got us two new boys today. I recon y'all know enough now since you dadden listen well. Y'all go over yonder and talk to them."

He points to two guys nearby, "That tall redhead boy is Wilson from down south. That dark-haired fellow is a Yankee like you from New York city."

Kenneth Wilson is tall, about 6', and has a funny way of walking on his toes. He has red hair and is always smiling. I walk up to him, "Hey Wilson where you from?" He says, "Hey, Y'all with that long name. I'm from down yonder in Clinton, North Carolina. It's a small city with mostly farm country. My kinfolk has a farm that I work with my three sisters and two brothers. I'm the youngest of the clan. We got that their name Clinton from some old boy, Henry Clinton, who had eleven ileginmitt children. We are all mostly southern, but the big cities have mostly Yankees.

"Yeah, my name is too long, you can call me Kirk. Do you have a weapon yet?"

"I'm fixin to carry that big old machine gun. I'm happy as a tick on a dog to kill me some Viet Cong. All moanin I've ate so much that I'm fixin to pop. Y'all know where we can get some women?"

"You might want to try up at the village. They have some nice, numbered woman you might like.

Wilson leaves and says, "Bless your heart. I'm gonna wonder over yonder and see me one of those numbered gals."

Pasquale Tizzio has the chiseled look of a boxer. He's handsome with dark features, is Italian and from New York city.

"Hey Tizzio, I'm Fred Kirkpatrick, you can call me Kirk. I see you're one of the new guys. Did they give you a weapon yet?"

"I hear I'm going to get the M-16 and also get to carry the radio."

I continue, "I hear you are from New York. Do you have a big family."

"Yeah, I'm from Noo Yowk. I only have a sister, but unlike you, she is young and beautiful."

We both laugh and I say, "I was born June 3, 1947. When were you born."

He laughs and says, "My sister's birthday is June 3. My birthday is May 3, 1947, so I'm way older and smarter than you."

I say, "You must be pretty smart to be getting the radio."

"I went to Our Lady of Mount Carmel Church, played football, and wore #66 in honor of Green Bay Packer great Ray Nitschke."

A few weeks later, Tizzio comes up to me. "Hey Kirk, I need your opinion on something. I've been noticed by the Battalion Commander, and he wants me to be one of his RTO's, but I ain't doin it. I don't think that 'a good idea."

I said to Tizzio, "Are you kidding, that is a very sweet deal since you will never on the ground. You got to take that position. I will be much safer for you, and you won't have to hump the boonies like us Infantrymen." Tizzio smiles, "Ahrite ahready, I'm gonna do it and get outta hea and visit my cousin Frankie in Lawn Guyland when I get home."

Operation Billings - June 16 to June 26, 1967. Our battalion, in conjunction with the 1st Battalion, 16th Infantry, is to move by foot, from LZ Rufe to position LZ X-Ray, a distance of a mile and a half. At 0800 hours the first elements, consisting of 1st Battalion, 16th Infantry (Alpha & Bravo companies) and Bravo company of the 2/28th, departed LZ Rufe. At 1255 hours, 2/28th's Bravo and 1/16th's Alpha companies are receiving heavy automatic and small arms fire.

Back at LZ Rufe, my company, is instructed to stay put. It is deemed too dangerous for us to move towards LZ X-Ray. The last CH-47 Chinook is airborne with the final supplies. As soon as the Chinook leaves, the VC begin a rocket attack on our position along with harassing sniper fire. The attack lasts for nearly one hour and we suffer twelve casualties.

It was almost as if the VC knew exactly where our forces would be landing that day. I remember being told before the start of missions to never tell anyone when we're leaving LaiKhe. I'm sure the numbered girls back at LaiKhe were probing for this information before we left.

Our company is now all by themselves in a very isolated spot. It feels like we are isolated from the world. We are told that we will be here, alone, for a few days and nights. We dig in and form our NDP. The area is about the size of a football field with many trees that are about 30-60 feet tall. There are a few open spots that don't contain trees.

We have our command area on the east side. The north side is used by our mortar platoon. My platoon, 3rd platoon, is on the south end. On our west is a lake, oval shaped, that occupies nearly twenty-five percent of our football size area. On the other side of the water, it's a large body of water, it looks man-made, is a small clearing. Behind that clearing are more trees. The water is not very deep, no more than three feet deep.

Around an hour later, Sgt. Condor leads a squad of his men out for an ambush detail. They are to cross the west side water area and setup on that small clearing. It's a potentially very dangerous move since they will be in the water, make noise, and be vulnerable to VC if they are waiting on the other side. Throughout the night, Sgt. Condor keeps detecting movement.

Around 1am, Sgt. Condor felt the movement was too close and sets off the ambush. Many rounds of ammo are being fired into the west area. The moon is out and its very bright on that end of the jungle. If Charlie didn't know we were here, he sure knows it now. Sgt. Condor and his squad make a hasty retreat across the large body of water.

Back at the NDP, Captain Burke and Sgt. Condor are having a heated discussion. Captain Burke wants Sgt. Condor to go back out and setup the ambush again. Sgt. Condor refuses to go out again saying that would be a suicide mission since the VC could be waiting behind the trees.

Captain Burke tells Condor that if he doesn't go back out, he will bust Condor down one rank to a Corporal. Sgt. Condor still refuses. Captain Burke comes up with a new plan. He has decided that I should take the squad out which I agree to do.

It's now close to 2AM and there is a very bright moon out. Crossing the water, I have the guys spread out so as not make it too easy if Charlie is on the other side. My thoughts are now on getting back home.

Crossing the river, I'm thinking, "*Up to this point of my tour in Vietnam, I have survived six months of jungle warfare. The name of the game has been to stay alive as long as possible. Now that looks like a long shot. I have to be super careful as we cross the open water.*"

On the other side of the water, we start setting up. I take a Claymore mine out a few yards, into the jungle area. As I'm about to place the Claymore into the ground, my heart stops. I can feel hairs growing up from inside my head. My throat is dry. Knots are in my stomach. My heart is beating faster than a cheetah running at full speed.

Looking down, I see a fresh Ox-Cart trail. The VC have just been here. No wonder Sgt. Condor set off his ambush. The VC must be very close. I know we are all in deep trouble. I hurry back to my squad to tell them.

I want to send out some M-79 rounds, but I decide that might be too risky. So, I decide to call in a "Fire Mission" and have our mortar platoon send out a few mortar rounds. The first round comes in about a hundred yards in front of us. I further adjust the rounds to my left and right, another hundred yards out. We can hear movement; it appears to be moving away from us.

The next morning, I lead the squad back from a long sleepless night. Captain Burke comes up to me and says, "Great Job Kirk. I'm putting you in for the Legion of Merit medal. And I'm going to make you a squad leader."

I'm not sure what a Legion of Merit medal is but becoming a squad leader was very good news. I know that within a few months, I could be promoted to Sgt E-5 with a chance to make Staff Sgt (E-6) before my tour is up.

The next morning, we are exploring the west section where we had all the movement. We find trees that have slits cut into them. These slits are about three feet off the ground. These slits are used to burn oil at night. This allows the VC to light their way as they move at night on the trail.

We find communication wire in the ground. The wire leads into Cambodia and turns out to be a major supply route from Cambodia to Saigon. It was a very ingenious method of movement since our planes couldn't spot the light.

We were back in LaiKhe only a few days, when the word came out that our battalion, would be adding a new company known as Delta by the end of July 1967. This new addition will be made up of newly arrived stateside group, known as C Packet, a group of about 100 men. They are on a ship bound for Vietnam and will arrive around mid-July.

It's the beginning of August and I'm heading over to my new assignment, 3rd platoon, 3rd squad. I'm very pleased to find that Gerald Thompson will be my squad leader. I consider Gerald an excellent leader and I will be his assistant. Our tent houses third platoon, third squad.

Also in our tent are two other guys that are not in our squad. Harry Marino, transferred from Bravo company and Wilbert Peters, from Mobile, Alabama. They are both weightlifters and it shows.

Gerald is from Maryville, Tennessee (pronounced Mare-a-ville by us yanks). We were together in Fort Polk, LA for advanced training. Gerald was my squad leader then.

He yells over to me, "Hey Fred, y'all come on over here."

Hey Gerald, how you doing?"

"Ah-rite. I want y'all to meet the rest of our squad over yonder. We got us eight out nine new guys.

"Donnie Hodges, a good old boy from down yonder in Texas is near as old as my grand pappy at twenty-seven. Frank MacMeel will be my RTO.

Y'all know Wilson, he's gonna carry the machine gun. That Black fellow is Richard Jones. He ain't but 18 yr. old, but I ain't worried about him. He boxed in them their Golden Gloves. I can't think right off where he's from, somewhere in Illinois.

That quiet boy with the M-79 is Gary Lincoln, from E-ton Ohio. He doesn't talk much even though he's nearly twenty-three.

Jack Schroder is another new boy. He's from Clay Center, Nebraska. If y'all have teeth problems, he can fix y'all cause he's studying dentistry. He got a new wife and six-month son down yonder so we gonna watch over him. He will be part of the machine gun crew as an ammo bearer.

I'm fixin to go fetch me a co-cola, why don't y'all go meet the rest of the squad."

Reynolds Lonefight says, "I'm a full-blooded American Indian. We can talk later. I'm heading to the village to see my girlfriend, #22."

Last I saw #22, she was very pregnant. Reynolds will carry the M-16 rifle and walk behind me when I walk point.

Wilson greets me, "Howdy Kirk, I'm fixin to go yonder to the off-limits village later. I'm waiting till it's dark and then I'm going to the off-limits village. I got to have some."

My good friend from Charlie is crazy, happy all the time and more than fearless. He can't just go the normal route for women. He has to go to the Off-limit village which is much more dangerous.

"Wilson, you know there are VC in that village and our Military Police (MPs) are all over that place. I'm going with you to guard your ass."

Emil Megiveron, from Pontiac, Michigan, just turned twenty on August 11. I ask him, "How you doing."

He says, "My sister Mary is very close to me and didn't want me to leave for Vietnam. She fears I won't come back. She begged me to go over to Canada, but I wasn't gonna do that. I'm the first born of nine children. My grandfather is part Native American, and my mother is an Indian Princess."

I said, "Wow. How cool is that. What did you before the Army?"

"I worked for General Motors, the Pontiac division, but during the weekends, I caddy for rich doctors who tip very well." "Well, you stay close to me in the field so you can get back to your sister Mary."

Ronney Reece won't be nineteen until November 25th. He is very quiet and shy. He will be the assistant machine-gunner to Wilson. I say to Reece, "Where you from?"

"I-I-I'am from Et Lanna, Georgia. I ain't never heared of Vietnam til just recent."

I realize that he has a stuttering problem and maybe that is why he is so quiet and shy. I make it my mission to try and help him and get him home safe.

Shenandoah II - October 7, 1967 - October 18, 1967, [13]: Operation Shenandoah II begins with General Hay, commanding general of the First Infantry Division, sending two brigades, the first and third brigades' of 1400 men, into the middle of this very dangerous region to prevent the 271st VC Regiment of 1200-1500 men from escaping the Long Nguyen Secret Zone.

The third brigade will operate in the south and the east. The First Brigade, commanded by Colonel George Newman, will operate in the northern and western portions. Included in the First Brigade is our elite 2nd Battalion, 28th Infantry.

The 2nd Battalion of the 28th Infantry Regiment is probably the best known and most elite unit of the First Infantry Division. The 2/28th regiment can trace their lineage of bravery back to World War I. In 1917, they were the first American combat unit to set foot on European soil. The regiment distinguished itself by conducting the first offensive operation by U. S. troops in World War I at the town of Cantigny.

---

13   Notes from Bravo Company Commander Captain Jim Kasik - http:// freepages. military. rootsweb. ancestry. com/~realmccoy/shenii. html

In a violent three-day battle, the regiment attacked the German-held French village of Cantigny. They captured Cantigny and withstood five German counter attacks. From that day forward, they were known as the "Lions of Cantigny." Because of our regimental patch, we are known as the "Black Lions." [14]

Normally the "Black Lions" are under the operational control of the 3rd brigade, but for this mission we are assigned to the First brigade and will be under the command of Colonel Newman.

Colonel Newman is new to Vietnam, having just arrived on September 12

The "Black Lions' are led by LTC Terry Allen Jr. He is the son of Major General Terry Allen Sr, who had led the First Infantry Division through some of the heaviest fighting in World War II.

LTC Allen Jr, just assumed command of the battalion in early August.

At the chopper pads, the nearly 400 helicopters, will transport the battalion into the jungles of the Long Nguyen Secret Zone, about twelve miles to the northwest of LaiKhe. I'm on the first of Twenty-five choppers that take the first load of Delta company to within a mile of the landing zone. Here we wait for the entire battalion to join us.

Waiting for us is a small army of print and television journalists waiting to film and interview the Black Lions since this is expected to be a "Hot Landing Zone." One of those reporters is a tall, attractive female in a black jumpsuit. They are filming for a show called "Shenandoah II", to be released in San Francisco, California, sometime late 1967 or early 1968.

I'm with six from my squad, waiting for choppers to transport us into the landing zone. The reporter moves to interview me.

She says to me, "Hello soldier, can you tell me your name and where you are from?"

---

14   The History of the 2nd Battalion, 28th Infantry, www. coachwyatt. com/blhistory. htm

"I'm Fred Kirkpatrick from Cleveland, Ohio and Delta's point man."

As she begins to ask me another question, choppers in the horizon are moving to land and transport us about a mile away, to the jungle area known as the Long Nguyen Secret Zone. As the choppers near, shots ring out from that jungle area. The choppers land and I take off on a dead run to the chopper with the others following in the same John Wayne Gung Ho manner.

As I walk point, I'm think to myself, what a beautiful day it is. The temperature is in the 90's and the air is very still. Ahead of me and to my right and left, are beautiful green leaves on very tall trees that are nearly 100 feet tall. As still as everything appears, I have the eerie feeling that someone is watching me.

I look down at my compass and continue walking at a very brisk pace as I keep scanning the trees for movement. As I quicken the pace, the rest of the company is almost running, trying to catch up with me. We get to the NDP site without any incident. The LZ turned out to not be hot to the chagrin of the press and they leave that evening on the resupply Chinooks.

OCTOBER 8: Not much happens on this day. We are clearing fields of fire and digging in. Single company and platoon size patrols go out in the area. We find a small cache of rice on a patrol.

OCTOBER 9: Just after 6 a. m. , our squad of eleven men led by Gerald Thompson, walks into the NDP. We have been on ambush patrol all night.

Since our squad was on ambush patrol, we will not go out with Delta this morning.

At 7AM, Delta and Bravo companies leave the NDP on a search-and-destroy mission. Delta is leading with Bravo following. Delta's 1st platoon, led by Sgt Mike Stubbs. As Stubbs moves about a couple hundred meters in the jungle, they walk up upon four VCs getting ready to cut some wood. The VC are surprised. They have no weapons and start running down a trail.

They move a short distance when one VC jumps out in front of point man Jackie Bolen Jr. who opens fire and kills the VC. An intense firefight begins. Fifty VC in trenches directly in front of Stubbs are firing. Another 10 VC are in trees above them. The bullets are knocking down leaves and bark off trees and kicking up so much dust that a cloud of dirt forms all around.

A VC nearby blows a claymore mine that seriously wounds RTO Ron Clark and renders the radio useless. Doug Ikerd is shot several times. The Vietnamese scout is hit in the leg. Larry Beckwith, the machine gunner, is hit in the leg. Stubbs is hit in the face with shrapnel from the claymore. Stubbs is hit in the neck while returning fire in the direction of the rifle flash, killing the VC. Welch and the rest of Delta have moved up.

Delta breaks contact, counting 13 dead VCs. The wounded are evacuated swiftly. Delta suffers six wounded in action, all of them from the 1st Platoon. Their injuries are serious, and none will return for the rest of this mission or any other mission. Delta is ordered back to the NDP. [15]

An hour later, Bravo company, goes back about 200 meters east of the original contact. They run into the VC. The point man from Bravo, Spec 4 William Anderson, is shot through the chest at point blank range and dies before a dust-off chopper could get in.

William Anderson becomes the first man to be lost to enemy during Operation Shenandoah II.

OCTOBER 10: Alpha Company and Recon Platoon conduct patrols east of the preceding contact on October 9. At 1305 and 1432 hours, Alpha finds 50 lbs. of rice, 12 bunkers, bloody clothing, 100-200 rounds, two grenades, two rockets, and fresh tracks.

---

15   Mike Stubbs, 2/28th Delta account of the battle he gave me about October 9, 1967. Stubbs wrote account in April 1972

OCTOBER 11: Bravo leading with Delta Company trailing, leave for a search-and-destroy mission at 8AM. An hour later, Bravo company, led by Captain Jim Kasik, after walking through dense jungle, comes upon a huge base camp. It was recently used, in good condition, but not occupied.

I'm leading Delta and come up behind Bravo company. On my left, I see a huge crater about 40 to 50 feet deep created from a bomb dropped in the area. A dog handler and his German Shepherd are walking around the area. I watch the dog sniff at the 500 lb bomb and decide it's time to leave that area.

I arrive at the massive base camp. The base camp is five football fields long by five football fields wide. I stop to look at one of the two-man bunkers. I say to myself, "These VC sure know how to make a bunker." It's the best-constructed bunker I've ever seen. It has taken a direct hit and is still standing.

I keep walking for what seems like hours and see bunker after bunker. I'm thinking, "What the hell are we doing here. The whole Viet Cong army must be here, and we are in the middle of their base camp. The place reminds me of Jack and the Beanstalk and that we are in the middle of the giants den."

This is the most dangerous area I've been to see since I arrived in Vietnam. I feel uneasy as I continue to walk through the Giant's Den.

Later that afternoon, the 1-18 infantry, makes a significant probe near the center of the Long Nguyen Secret Zone. The Viet Cong tries to lure the 1-18th infantry into a "trap", but with the help of a scout dog and their point man, they avoid the ambush and hit the 271st with artillery and gunships.

OCTOBER 12: Delta, Recon, and Alpha go back to that large base camp we found on October 11. LTC Allen is on the ground for the first time. A medic is looking at a sore on Allen's ankle that has been giving him problems. I see my buddy Tizzio and stop to chat. Tizzio is now LTC Allen's RTO and loves his new job.

OCTOBER 13: After six days of search-and-destroy missions in the Nguyen Secret Zone, the decision is made to relocate our base camp several kilometers to the north and east along the Ong Thanh Stream. Our battalion moves out early in the morning. It's a walk-through hell with temps in the high 90's and very high humidity. A few minutes later it starts raining as we continue to walk for close to four miles. It rains most of the trip.

Later that night, we spend hours digging our foxholes. Then we pull guard duty with two men on guard at each foxhole (two hours on duty, two hours off). My partner tonight is Gary Lincoln. Gary is taking about his religion and his family back home in Ohio. Gary says to me, "What religion are you, Kirk?"

"I'm Catholic but haven't been to church lately, but I'm needing God more than ever. My mother sent me this rosary I wear around my neck all the time. She had it blessed by the Pope and so far, has been very lucky for me."

We stay up most of the night talking and Gary is very much at peace tonight. During the night, we can hear the VC moving near our position. They are so close that I can almost hear them breathing. I want to throw a grenade at them in the worst way. But I know I can't give away our position, so we sit and wait.

OCTOBER 14: It's early morning and I'm up early to catch a chopper to Bien Hoa and then on to Japan. There are five to six others waiting for the chopper to come into the NDP. Among them is Roy Key, who is going with me to Japan and Larry Hammons, a friend of Gerald Thompson, who is headed to Australia.

I walk over to my squad to say goodbye. I talk briefly with Lincoln, Wilson, Schroder, Megiveron, and Lonefight. Nearby is Reece, I walk towards him and say, "Thought for sure you'd get that R & R and we'd go to Australia. You should have gotten that R & R instead of me since you've never had one. Reece doesn't look right, and I say to him, "You look nervous, what's wrong?"

"K-K-Kirk, I'm scared out here, I wish I was leaving with you". I say, "You'll be fine, just stay out of the killing zone if the shit hits the fan. Tell you what, loan me $10 and I'll give it back to you in a about a week when I get back." Reece "loans" me the symbolic $10. The idea was to make Reece comfortable knowing I will return in a week and give him back the $10.

October 15: Vietnam Long Nguyen Secret Zone. Bravo company and Recon platoon, on a patrol South of the new NDP, discover a spooky looking trail that consists of broken saplings to your left and right. It appears to be a marker system by the VC to travel at night. They follow the trail for a distance and come to a larger, more prominent trail. Soon three VC appear walking north. Recon opens fire and kills one VC.

OCTOBER 15: Army NCO Club – Bien Hoa, VIETNAM

It is late night and Hammons; Key and I are drinking as we wait for connecting flights. I write Thompson to have him keep an eye on the new guys. [16]

"To the baddest squad leader in Delta Company:

Hello Dude, how's the infantry life going? I just got out of LaiKhe today. Had to wait one and half days. I'm going to Camp Alpha tomorrow and then out to Japan the same day. I've been in the NCO club most of today and the rest of the time in the EM club. I'm about half drunk now. Hope you guys are staying out of trouble.

I'd sure hate to come back and find no squad."

October 16: Roy Key and I arrive at the R & R center, Camp Zama, in Japan, on October 16. I will be able to sleep well for the next five days knowing Gerald is watching over our squad.

---

16   Gerald Thompson sent me letter I wrote to him, postmarked October 16, 1967 from Japan

October 16: Vietnam Long Nguyen Secret Zone. Delta company is leading, and Bravo is trailing as they move on a southeastern direction as they conduct a search-and-destroy mission. They catch the VC by surprise and get into a major firefight that goes nearly perfect for the two companies. They kill at least twenty-one VC. [17]

The brigade and battalion command believe they are very close to the vital organ of the 271st VC Regiment and a BIG VICTORY is within their grasp. THEY WANT BLOOD. Colonel Newman wants Allen to be on the ground on October 17 to lead two companies for this victory. They will head due South, an azimuth of 180 degrees, to destroy the Viet Cong. However, there are some danger signs, that they are ignoring:

Clark Welch, Delta commander, is warning that going South is the only direction that has not been taken, making it the obvious direction the Viet Cong will expect them to take. Vietnamese Irregulars, who have been working with Welch since October 8, are warning that "Beaucoup VC are out there." The Vietnamese are terrified of the area and all of them leave the night of October 16, an ominous sign of the shedding of blood.

You never let your guard down in Vietnam or death could be certain.

---

17   James Shelton's S3 files of Statistical Summary of Operations, October 16, 1967

CHAPTER 5

The Battle of Ong Thanh

(October 17, 1967)

"When just near the dawn of victory, many will pause and second guess themselves."

--- Tite Kubo

I'm enjoying my R & R in Japan not knowing the danger my battalion is about to face today. Soon my world will change, and I will never recover from it.

The night of October 16, Colonel Newman and LTC Allen, agreed to setup a few airstrikes for the October 17 march to the enemy's rear to discourage the VC from trying to escape to the south. [18] They both knew artillery marching fire was the main deterrent to VC assaults, so it was decided that Major Sloan, Operations Officer (S3), would stay in the NDP at the Tactical Operations Center (TOC), to have artillery zeroed in with marching fire. [19]

---

18   James Shelton, The Beast Was Out There, page 126

19   James Shelton, The Beast Was Out There, page 217

Marching fire in front of the company, as they move forward is done for two reasons: To discourage the enemy from setting up an ambush and establish coordinates to place artillery on the enemy.

The senior officers of the 1st Infantry were very confident they could destroy their formidable enemy. They would march due South on October 17, a move that would put them directly in front of the suspected enemy base camp.

This overconfidence led to several errors:

The top brass from the 1st Infantry were aware that a large regiment was probably in the Long Nguyen Secret Zone, but their intelligence estimated the enemy force at no more than 400, but the enemy strength was closer to 1500 men. [20]

Colonel Newman, who had been commander of the 1st Brigade for less than a month, [21] ordered LTC Allen to be on the ground on October 17. Newman believed that the battalion commander should accompany their men in the jungle. LTC Allen preferred to supervise the action from a helicopter.

Colonel Newman's decision is a major blunder

Newman's decision to have Allen on the ground created several problems: Allen would not be in the air to coordinate artillery and air support, and his RTOs with their long whip antennas, could be spotted easily by VC snipers and attract fire like magnets early in a firefight.

07:30 hours: Alpha and Delta companies, along with the nine-man battalion group, begin to gather at the Night Defensive Perimeter (NDP).

An NDP is like a home away from home when you are out in the jungle.

---

20   Terry Tibbetts, A Spartan Game, page 229

21   James Shelton, The Beast Was Out There, page 203

Alpha and Delta are well below their normal combat strength of 100 to 120 men per company. These 155 men will shortly begin an exhausting toil deep into the Long Nguyen Secret Zone to look for the enemy.

Every minute of the march, you had to be careful to avoid punji pits, booby traps, and signs of an enemy presence. You can never relax.

08:02 hours: With high humidity and temperatures in excess of 90 degrees, Alpha company leads out as they march due south. Clifford Lynn Breeden is the point man for Alpha company and the entire Battalion. Behind the twenty-five-man 1st platoon, is the seven-man Alpha command group led by Captain George. His two RTO's Lee Price and Michael Farrell are followed by FO Paul Kay and his RTO James Jones. Trailing them is Army lifer, 1st Sgt Jose Valdez.

In two-company patrols, the lead company sets the pace of the march, can vary from the planned march, and have priority on artillery support. Paul Kay, Alpha FO, is calling in artillery marching fire. Most of the fire is directed in front of Alpha (South), 300-400 meters ahead. [22]

The 2nd platoon, with only twenty-two men, is led by jungle savvy point man, 25-year-old Allan Reilly. The trailing 3rd platoon, with only eleven men, is commanded by 2nd Lt. Thomas Mullen Jr.

No planned B-52 strikes on the night of October 16, are ever made.

08:55 hours: F-100's and B-57 Canberra's flies the 1st of preplanned airstrikes to the southeast and southwest against suspected enemy base camps of the 271st VC Regiment. A 2nd airstrike follows at 0910 hours. But due to faulty intelligence, their bombs hit in an empty jungle, many meters from where the 271st VC Regiment is located. [23]

09:20 hours: Nearly ninety minutes later, Delta Company with 81 men moves out of the NDP. Delta's twenty-seven-man 3rd platoon is

22   James Jones, RTO for FO Paul Kay, interview by Captain Cash

23   Clark Welch interview by Captain Cash

the lead platoon. The 3rd platoon, because of their overall experience, is generally regarded as the best platoon in the company. Delta is on a much faster pace as Delta's point man Reynolds Lonefight, hurries to maintain visual contact with Alpha's rear platoon.

Delta's eight-man Company group is led by Clark Welch who has more combat experience than any officer in the battalion. He is considered by many to be the best company commander in the battalion. Walking with Welch and Barrow are Welch's two RTOs, Paul Scott, and Jimmy Scott. Also in the Delta command group are Forward Observer Harold "Pinky" Durham, with his RTO Joseph Booker.

Behind the Delta command group is Delta's twenty-two 2nd platoon, led by Texas sharpshooter Staff Sgt. Dwayne Byrd. Behind Delta's 2nd platoon, is the nine-man Battalion command group of LTC Terry Allen.

Several in the Battalion group look out of place in the jungle with their neatly starched fatigues and highly polished boots. Surely that gives them away as important targets for the waiting Viet Cong.

The 1st platoon, with twenty-four men, is the rear platoon, commanded by 2Lt. Andrew Luberta, who has only been in country a few days. On the 1st platoon's right flank is the 3rd squad, named "Lucky 13" since they are the 1st platoon, 3rd squad. David Halliday is the very last man in Delta company's formation.

As the 155-man group leaves the NDP, none of them notice several VC snipers high above in the trees looking down on them as they move.

Alpha is moving at a very slow and overly cautious pace, traveling no more than five hundred meters in forty-five minutes. The unnecessary clover leafing every 100-200 meters is slowing them down.

Since the jungle is made up of thousands of miles of land, the smarter choice might have been to look for clear danger signs such as trails or VC base camps.

09:56AM hours: After traveling only 1000 meters in two hours, Cliff Breeden comes across what looks like a highway in the jungle. It's a huge well-used trail on a diagonal that runs southwest to northwest. There are fresh sandal prints running both ways that have been made within the hour.

There are also freshly cut trees, a huge danger sign that VC are very close by.

During training at Fort Polk, LA, we were taught, "NEVER WALK ON A TRAIL" since that increases your exposure to booby traps, or worse, an enemy ambush.

Breeden immediately recognizes the danger and stops the formation to talk with Johnson about the trail. Willie C. Johnson, the 1st platoon leader, calls Captain George and they decide to investigate the trail by sending cloverleaf patrols on each side to the trail.

Cliff Breeden with the 2nd squad's nine men led by Randy Brown, take the west route. Ray Gribble's 1st squad of nine men, take the north route. Willie C. Johnson and his RTO Buentiempo walk behind the 2nd squad. Platoon leader Pipkin, his RTO and two medics, follow behind Gribble's squad.

As Gribble is taking his squad across the trail, he sees movement and reports back to Johnson. Breeden had not moved more than 75 yards before he detects one VC on the trail walking westerly. The lone VC is now followed by a group of six or seven VCs. Johnson reports this to Captain George, who tells them to form a hasty ambush.

At Fort Polk, LA, we were told to not fall for VC traps if they suddenly appeared on trails out of nowhere, they are trying to draw you deeper into a trap.

Alpha is being drawn into a trap of no return.

They wait in place for nearly fifteen. Then Johnson says to Gribble, "The trees are moving, and I think someone is in them." Gribble and James Schultz hear "the clicking of bolts and the rattle of ammunition in metal containers." [24] George instructs the 2nd squad to move up slightly to the left of the 1st squad.

This moves to set up an ambush inside of a potential VC trap, reminded me of a classic scene from "Butch Cassidy and The Sundance Kid". Newman and Redford are cornered by an entire regiment of Bolivian troops but are unable to comprehend the reality of their doomed situation. The two come out blazing for a planned dash towards their horses. What they don't know is that hundreds of rifles are trained on them. Escape is impossible, death is certain.

10:15 hours: Just as Breeden and the 2nd squad are moving up, the quiet is broken by withering fire from 600 hundred hardcore Viet Cong attacking Alpha's 1st platoon.

The sound of the gunfire is deafening, like 100 jackhammers going off at the same time. You can get pain or ringing in your ears (tinnitus) after exposure to noise. Human speech registers at 25-35 decibels. Any sound above 85 decibels can cause hearing loss. The sound of a jackhammer can reach decibel levels of 130 decibels. Gunfire can approach decibels levels of 145-155 decibels. Imagine being at a gun range and 200 men firing their weapons at the same time and you don't have hearing protection. [25]

The attack comes from three directions, the southwest, west, and northwest. The twenty-five-man platoon is under heavy fire from bolt-action carbines, AK47 automatic rifles, and machine guns firing long bursts from well-camouflaged bunkers on the west.

Six claymore mines explode all around them. Snipers are raining fire down on them from trees. Machine gun fire increases, amid the sickening sounds of men screaming in pain as bullets pierce their

---

24   Combat After Action Report, dated March 31, 1968, freepages. military. rootsweb. ancestry. com/~realmccoy/afteract. html

25   Top 10 Loudest Noises - listverse. com/2007/11/30/top-10loudest-noises/

bodies. Some are calling for their mothers or moaning in pain unable to speak. Several are trying to dig into the ground with their fingers for some shelter. Medics are hurrying to the screams and moans of the wounded and dying.

Delta is receiving sporadic AK47 fire from approximately five VCs located in trees to the right flank of Delta company. They are quickly taken under fire, killed and fall about ten feet from the trees and dangle in midair, their legs strung up in vines. Welch then shifts the 3rd platoon, under 2nd Lt. David Stroup, to a right front direction in reaction to Alpha companies contact. [26]

Alpha has walked into the middle of a killing zone. A killing zone is an area that is entirely covered by enemy fire. Soldiers within this zone are isolated and trapped.

Cliff Breeden is shot from a sniper in the trees. Breeden lets out a blood-curdling scream of, "Ambush", and is hit again, and again and again. He fires his weapon on fully automatic into the trees as he becomes the 1st to die.

Directly behind Breeden, Jerry Lancaster, and Ralph Carrasco, quickly follow as the 2nd and 3rd in death, both killed from machine gun fire.

Randy Brown and his RTO Morrissette are wounded. Tears are running down Morrissette face as he is bleeding badly. John Henderson is hit by a sniper. Larry Hartman and his three-men machine gun crew are firing at the camouflaged bunker.

Wesley Dodson and Leon East from the machine gun crew are the 4th and 5th to die. Within a minute, Ray Gribble, the 6th to die, is killed from machine gun fire coming from the camouflaged bunkers. Larry Anderson, the 7th to die, is killed by a sniper.

Bodies of wounded and dead are bouncing up and down as rounds hit them, over and over. Body parts are flying everywhere.

---

26   SP4 Williams interview of Clark Welch on October 20, 1967

Ken Anderson and Ronald Courts are wounded. Ken Anderson is yelling, "I'm hit. I'm hit, help me I don't want to die here." Courts is struggling to breathe.

A VC comes running out from behind a tree towards Willie Johnson. The VC hits him with a burst of four rounds just below the heart. Johnson falls back and hits the ground. Blood is pouring out from his leg and chest. Valdez ties his handkerchief around his leg. [27]

One of the rounds goes through Johnson and hits his RTO Buentiempo. Medic Allen Jagielo comes up and stops Johnson's bleeding but is shot through the heart by a sniper and becomes the 8th to die. The other medic John Abraham, is wounded, as is Ronald Whetistine.

Larry Hartman is firing his M-60 machine gun. Paul Fitzgerald and Olin Hargrove are returning fire from their M-16's. There is total confusion. Soldiers are running and crawling. Soldiers are yelling in pain. Others are crying, "Mama, Mama." The smell of dead bodies is too much for some as they throw up their breakfast.

Donald Pipkin and his RTO Michael Arias, move up to help. Pipkin sees movement in trees to his left, fires at the tree, a AK-47, followed by a VC, drops from the tree. Pipkin is shot in the left leg.

Arias yells into the radio to George, "Get help to us now, were in an ambush." A VC sees Arias and shoots up his radio so that it no longer works. Pipkin starts dragging Ken Anderson to safety. Pipkin gets about 10 feet on his own until James Schultz comes to help and drags both Pipkin and Ken Anderson to a safe area.

Larry Puyea and James Schultz, from the 1st squad, fire as they take cover behind trees. Clarence Rorie, also in the squad, crawls to a tree. His hands are trembling as he fires M-79 rounds at the bunkers.

The jungle is quickly filled with the faces of death. In less than five minutes, Alpha's 1st Platoon's twenty-five-man unit is nearly wiped out as eight are killed and ten others are wounded in action.

---

27   1st Sgt. Jose Valdez interview by Fred Kirkpatrick on 3/13/04

LTC Allen and his command group have taken cover behind a large anthill. Allen tells Welch, "Form a two-platoon perimeter with your 1ˢᵗ and 2ⁿᵈ platoons around the command group. Your third platoon is to stay in contact with Alpha."

10:20 hours: Alpha's 2nd platoon, under 2LT Peter Edwards, moves up to help the 1st platoon. They are deployed online to the right of the 1ˢᵗ platoon. Edwards and his RTO Kelly Jenkins, move forward with the 1ˢᵗ squad to the left, facing west. The 2nd squad led by Carl Woodard and his RTO Roger Baldwin, follow closely behind. The entire 2nd platoon is quickly pinned down by heavy fire pouring into both flanks from a Browning . 50 caliber machine gun in a concealed bunker.

The Browning . 50 caliber machine gun was originally developed during World War I and can effectively hit targets as far away as 1,800 meters. The bullet can tear a man in half and cause horrible dismemberment of limbs. If the bullet hits your head, it will obliterate most, if not all of the entire skull. [28]

The 2nd squad is under intense fire. Allan Reilly, the 9th to die, as he advances towards the bunker. Richard Crites, Arturo Garcia, and John Krische, killed trying to take out the machine gun, become the 10th, 11th, and 12th to die.

Edwards throws a grenade at the machine gun position and is hit in the right arm by a round. Blood is oozing out of his arm. RTO Kerry Jenkins and David Esary, the platoon sergeant, are also wounded. Roger Baldwin, Woodard's RTO, is wounded.

The machine gun crew of Eddie Mitchell and Robert Brown are wounded but manage to take out the . 50 caliber machine gun. Doc Hinger spots a sniper in the tree and points him out to Costello who lobes grenades from his M79 into the trees killing the VC. Costello is wounded at the top of his left shoulder by a grenade. Hinger is slightly wounded by the blast.

---

28   Troops love the . 50 caliber, www. wearethemighty. com/articles/m2-50-cal-machine-gun

VC snipers and VC machine guns open up on the 1st squad from the immediate front. They are getting heavy fire, explosions from claymores are blown, and grenades are thrown at them. Santos Camero becomes the 13th to die. Grenadier Michael Gallagher, killed from machine gun fire, is the 14th.

The seven remaining men retreat towards Delta's 3rd platoon. As they retreat, they are running, stumbling, and crawling to avoid fire because Delta thinks they are VC. Now both Delta and the VC are shooting at them. Bullets are ripping through their bodies. All are wounded and crawl towards Delta yelling, "Don't shoot, we're Alpha." Delta realizes the error and lets them into the area. [29]

Alpha's twenty-two-man 2nd platoon is nearly wiped out as six are killed and fifteen others are wounded in action. All that remains of Alpha's sixty-five-man company is the seven-man command group and eleven-man 3rd platoon.

10:25 hours: Captain George, unable to communicate with either the 1st or 2nd platoon leaders, moves forward with his six-man command group, to a machine-gun nest that has Alpha's 1st and 2nd platoons pinned down. His group throws a flurry of grenades at the machine-gun nest, silencing it, but gives their position away. Another VC machine gun turns it fire on the command group and George opens up with his CAR-15 rifle and takes out the machine gun.

At 10:30 hours: A VC soldier dashes out of a bunker, running at the command group with a 36" Chinese claymore mine. The VC attempts to set up the mine directly in front of them, but instead places the mine off to an angle. The VC starts running back and Jerry Price kills him. However, another VC is able to detonate the mine. There is a very big explosion that blows the VC to pieces and tears a tree, about two feet around, into pieces. Soldiers are moaning and screaming, "Medic, Medic."

---

29   Combat After Action Report, dated March 31, 1968, freepages. military. rootsweb. ancestry. com/~realmccoy/afteract. html

Medics Archie Porter, Tom Hinger, and Jim Norgon, run up to help. [30]

Claymore mines use a curved block of C-4 explosive. A large number of pellets are embedded in the face of the explosive, creating a shocking blast of fragments comparable to the effect of an oversized shotgun. The explosive burns with intense heat. [31]

Michael Farrell, who is just left of the tree, takes the brunt of the blast and is instantly killed, becoming the 15th to die. His radio is smoking and no longer works.

Paul Kay, near the big tree, is knocked into semi-consciousness. Kay comes to and sees lots of blood coming from his arm and is able to stop the bleeding by applying a direct bandage. [32]

Jerry Price is hit on his right side but does not realize he has massive tissue wounds. He keeps firing until his M-16 rifle begins to melt down. [33]

Spent shrapnel from the blast lands near Valdez and hits PSG Johnson who yells, "I'm hit, Top." Valdez comes to Johnson's aid and sees he has welts on his arms from the blast.

Captain George is struck in the face, severely wounding his left cheekbone. His eyesight is reduced to a blur of silhouettes. The concussion ruptures his eardrum that leaves George nearly deaf. Price says to George, "You are badly hurt, and we have to move back." Price is able to drag Captain George back to an anthill near Valdez. Unable to see or hear very well, George tells Valdez to move the company back towards the NDP. George then calls LTC Allen and tells him, "I'm hit badly and trying to break contact."

---

30   Captain Cash interview of Tom Hinger on October 22, 1967

31   . Claymore, www. vietnamwar. net/claymore. htm

32   Fred Kirkpatrick interview on 3/13/2004 of Paul Kay, FO for Alpha Company

33   Fred Kirkpatrick interview of Jerry Price, CO RTO

James Jones, Kay's RTO, not hit during the blast, tries to move away, but a VC with an AK47 opens up on him and shoots the whip off his radio. Jones returns fire with his . 45 until its empty. Then he picks up Farrell's M-16 and fire it until it jams.

Delta's FO, Durham receives word on his radio that FO Kay has been wounded. Braving enemy fire, Durham, arrives and issues coordinating artillery instructions to Kay's RTO. As Durham moves back to the Delta area, he is severely wounded in the head, but is able to return to the Delta area.

As Jones lays on the ground, he is able to reach his artillery boss, Captain Suttle, on the radio and calls in a fire mission at the 1st Division Artillery Battery. The artillery comes in within 50 meters of his location. Jones is getting heavy shrapnel, but within five minutes, the constant pounding of three batteries of artillery slows the VC automatic fire enough for Jones to escape the area. [34]

10:35 hours: When the claymore mine exploded, 3rd platoon leader, Lt. Mullen, moved forward with his eleven-man platoon to help. After traveling not more than a few dozen meters, they are hit by a tremendous amount of fire. Mullen is hit in the right arm and loses consciousness.

Burchett, Duncan, Richard Hillstrom, Adolfo Martinez Gonzalez, and Allen King are all wounded. Squad leader, Steve Ellis, and the entire machine gun crew of Elwood Chaney, John Familiare, and Walter Platosz are all killed. They become the 16th, 17th, 18th, and 19th to die.

Mullen comes to and Adolfo Gonzalez is talking to him, "I can see the machine gun that hit you". Mullen is able to get a grenade off his harness and rolls it over to Gonzalez who takes the machine gun out, but they draw fire from a VC with an AK-47.

---

34   Captain Cash interview of James Jones on October 22, 1967

Mullen is hit a second time in both legs and arms and four of his fingers are shot off his hand. Mullen loses consciousness for a brief period of time.

Costello nearby is asking if anyone knows the battalion frequency. Mullen remembers the frequency but can't work his radio because of his hand, so he tells Costello the frequency. Costello is able to reach William Coleman and his three-man crew. They instruct Costello how to set up some type of defense perimeter and tell him that help is on the way. [35]

Platoon Sgt. David Duncan, his RTO Kelly Burchett, Hillstrom and King reach the ambush area. They are Joined by Delta's FO Pinky Durham and his RTO Joseph Booker. They find the dead have been field stripped naked of their weapons and gear and their throats have been slit.

Scattered all around the dead bodies are pieces of paper, slightly larger than a business size envelope. Printed on the paper is a black-and-white photograph of a body of an American soldier lying on a battlefield. Two lines of English are printed on the paper that reads:

Your X-Rays Have Come Back from The Lab, And I think I Know What Your Problem Is. [36]

They find Willie C. Johnson, with powder burns all over his body. He appears to be dead. Hillstrom is Yelling, "Hey, he's still alive." They put Johnson in a poncho and carry him away from the area.

Duncan gets separated from the group. Machine gun fire is directed at Duncan who jumps on the ground and lands on Thomas Bell. He says, "Get the fuck off me." This shocks Duncan and he gets up and sprints towards an anthill. In doing so, he is shot in the back, flipping him over. As he is laying on the ground, he is hit in the stomach.

---

35   Fred Kirkpatrick interview of Thomas Mullen Jr. on 1/16/2002

36   John Laurence, The Cat from Hue, page 388

Duncan attempts to get up and his leg is shot off by a rocket, throwing him in the air, while his leg flies in another direction. His ears are ringing from the blast. He's bleeding, lying behind an anthill as VC are walking all around him. His pulse is racing and the hairs on his head feel like they're growing. He's waiting to die. Suddenly a hand is on his shoulder. It's Thomas Bell, who says to Duncan, "You alive?" and hoists Duncan onto his back and carries him out. [37]

At 10:40 hours: Valdez is on the radio to Allen. "Sir, George and all platoon leaders are wounded." Allen tells Valdez, "You assume command and move Alpha to the northeast." Valdez following orders and moves with the battered remains of 1st platoon and the command group.

Within twenty minutes Alpha company is shattered. The company now is nothing more than stragglers on a full retreat east with Valdez or heading towards Delta company's area.

2nd Platoon hears Valdez yelling, "Come to the fire", as he shoots his .45 twice in the air. Peter Edwards, Kerry Jenkins, David Esary, William Brans, Carl Woodard, Roger Baldwin, Eddie Mitchell, and Roger Brown from the 2nd platoon, crawl towards him.

Arias on his way to the Valdez area is shot by a VC in a tree that hits his radio, knocking him down. He is yelling in terror, "I'm Hit." Joe Bailey from the 2nd platoon who's been shot in the shoulder, crawls over to discover that the bullet has only hit the radio. Bailey says to Arias, "Get up mother fucker. You're not hit."

Arias crawls away into a safe area close to the Valdez area. Tears start running down his face. He's trembling and scared to death that the VC will come and finish him off. Arias hears the others with Valdez and crawls to safety towards them.

---

37   Fred Kirkpatrick interview of David Duncan on 1/24/2004

Valdez has Fitzgerald and Hargrove go back to look for wounded. As they are searching, they get off track. Friendly artillery is exploding just over their heads. They start running but can't outrun artillery shells that land on them. They are blown to pieces, becoming the 20th and 21st to die.

In less than thirty minutes, Alpha company is nearly obliterated. The 65-man company suffers staggering losses of twenty-one killed and thirty-three wounded.

10:40 to 11:20 hours: LTC Allen is on the radio providing Situation Reports to Major John Sloan, who is back at the NDP in the tactical operations center. The situation on the ground is very intense as Allen requests artillery immediately.

Damn it Allen. Pull back! Save the rest of the Battalion.

Colonel Newman is second-guessing Allen's decisions and has artillery halted and requests air strikes instead. LTC Allen adamantly disagrees with the decision but is quickly overruled by his superior officer. [38]Lt. Col Allen has his command group stay in place adjacent to the prominent anthill.

One has to wonder why LTC Allen didn't pull back to the NDP during the long lull. Perhaps he was ordered to stay in place by Newman. [39]

Delta company waits patiently in place for the airstrikes to arrive. Delta expects they will be moving back to the NDP.

Colonel Newman has made a critical error by second-guessing Allen during the battle. By halting artillery fire to call for air strikes, there is a long lull, estimated to be as long as 45 minutes, in which there is no close fire support of any type from outside to the people on the ground. [40]

---

38   Captain Cash interview of Major John Sloan on October 22, 1967

39   Terry Tibbetts, A Spartan Game, page 234

40   Captain Cash interview of Major John Sloan on October 22, 1967

11:35 hours: During the 45-minute lull, the VC move very close to the Battalion command group. This tactic is called "Hugging the Enemy." By getting so close the VC have negated artillery and air strikes because of fear of friendly fire casualties. [41]

The VC quickly surround the remaining soldiers and the 2nd wave begins as 600 VC quickly attack Delta and make the Battalion CP area the second killing zone. The VC are now firing on all three sides of Delta and the Battalion group.

When the 2nd wave begins, Colonel Newman realizes his error and halts further air strikes and orders artillery to resume firing. The damage is done. It is too late!

Delta is receiving a heavy volume of fire from VC in trees with AK-47's and Carbines. VC are also firing claymores and RPGs from trees. Machine gun fire is coming from the ground on three sides, east, west, and south. The only way out is to retreat north, back to the NDP. They are firing down on Delta company and the battalion command group.

11:45 hours: Welch has Delta's nine-man 3rd squad, from the 3rd platoon, moves forward to help. They come under heavy fire from multiple machine guns. Donnie Hodges is wounded. Frank McMeel jumps behind a clump of bushes and tries to move, but a bullet goes through his C-rations. He looks down, sees blood, and is hit a 2nd and 3rd time.

Emil Megiveron and Richard Jones are receiving machine gun fire from several machine crews. They have hit them over and over. Megiveron and Jones are killed. They become the 1st to die from the Delta and the 22nd and 23rd to die.

---

41   Small Wars Journal - smallwarsjournal. com/blog/grab-their-belts-to-fight them

Gary Lincoln is firing his M-79 with devastating accuracy as he silences one VC machine gun position. However, the booming explosions and sounds are so loud, they increase his heart rate to an abnormal level. [42] His heart fails him, and he dies from a heart attack, becoming the 24th to die in the battle.

Reynolds Lonefight is firing away with his M-16 rifle and is wounded. The machine gun crew of Wilson, Reece, and Schroder direct crippling machine gun fire on the VC, killing several of them.

Reece is hit in the throat. He's spitting out blood. He's unable to move or talk and is the 25th to die. Schroder is shot in the leg but manages to crawl away to safety. Wilson is hit in both legs and arms. He's having a hard time breathing but continues to inflict heavy casualties on the advancing VC. A VC sniper shoots him in the head. Part of his head is missing, and he dies within seconds, becoming the 26th to die.

Within five minutes, my 3rd platoon's nine-man 3rd squad is destroyed. Five are killed and three are wounded. Jack Schroder is the only one in my squad that has not been killed or wounded.

11:50 hours: All four of Welch's radios have been damaged, so he has to crawl to the battalion command position to communicate with LTC Allen. As Welch gets close to the command area, he is struck by a VC machine gun that rips his left bicep off. Welch runs towards the machine gun and fires one shot with his . 45 caliber pistol and kills a VC who has penetrated the perimeter.

Another VC machine gun opens up on Welch with a long burst of fire that hits Welch's pistol slide. Welch is hit again in the left arm. Welch crawls towards the battalion command area and is hit four times in the back from a claymore blast.

---

42   Loud sounds - www. asha. org/public/hearing/noise/

Paul Scott immediately goes to Welch's aid through a hail of gunfire. He removes C-ration cans from a sock and uses the sock as a tourniquet that saves Welch's life. Welch is having trouble breathing. His arm is trembling. Paul Scott moves Welch to a tree where Welch passes out briefly.

As the enemy presses the 2nd attack, Durham calls for supporting artillery fire to be placed almost directly on his position, driving back the VC several times. He keeps adjusting on the artillery fires until he is essentially a target. As the artillery strikes get closer, Durham is sprayed by artillery.

A few minutes later, Durham is hit in the abdomen and blood is seeping from his wound. He then moves to a position in a small clearing, which offers a better vantage point, to adjust the fire. As he moves forward, a bullet blasts away his entire right hand. Durham is now calling artillery fire by operating his radio "press to talk" switch with a bloody stub where his hand had been.

A wounded Durham has ordered artillery fire very close to both the south and west sides of their position. The artillery fire is very close and very effective. Durham, talking on the radio, "I know I'm going to die, but I just want to tell you that the artillery fire is good, don't bring it in any closer."

1st Sergeant Barrow is about 10 yards from the battalion command group for the entire battle. A rocket explodes to Barrow's right rear and causes multiple fragment wounds to his left leg. He bites his lips in pain. Blood is pouring out of his leg. The explosion knocks Barrow out.

When he wakes up, he sees Delta's FO Durham, who is near death, raise himself up slightly and points to two VC with machine guns advancing to the command group. Durham yells, "Top". Durham dies a few minutes later, still holding the radio handset.

Harold Durham is the 27th to die.

The VC get within 15 meters of the command group and Barrow fires over Allen's head and kills the two advancing VC. Barrow, now on his last magazine, is looking for ammo for his M-16 when he sees a M-60 with ammo from a dead American machine gunner, probably Wilson.

He picks the weapon up and is then shot in both legs. Barrow turns and kills two VC who are running towards him as he leans against a tree. Barrow has blood all over him. It's not his blood, but the blood of the dead VC. VC are blowing claymore mines, sending in rocket-propelled grenades. Sniper fire is pouring down from VC in trees with AK-47's.

11:55 hours: A VC in a tree is firing at both sides of Bill McGath from the 3rd platoon. He is laying at an angle near a tree, so the VC sniper is unable to hit him. McGath calculates which of three trees the VC is in and shoots around the tree with one hand using his M-79. He fires a total of three rounds at the same tree. The third round blows the VC apart. McGath moves forward and finds the VC's foot lying on the ground.

Mike Kotowski, in the 3rd platoon, is hit in both legs and is pinned down and falls near Horace Williams. Both are lying flat. They can feel the bullets hit across their backs. Williams rolls to his side, facing Kotowski, as if he's ready to say something.

THERE IS AN EXPLOSION.

Horace Williams is Yelling, "I think I'm hit. I can't feel my legs. Can you see if they are still there?" Kotowski checks and sees his legs are still there. But Williams has lost his foot. It is dandling off his leg. Kotowski calls for a medic as he tries to stop the bleeding.

12:00 hours: The 3rd platoon, is receiving machine gun fire, in 50-100 round bursts, that is coming in six inches off the ground. Welch fixes the location of the machine gun and sends Gary Barker, Bob Nagy, and Stanley Gilbert to try and take out the machine gun. They move forward, shooting their M-16's as they advance.

Nagy and Gilbert are killed. Barker sees the VC machine gun that is inflicting casualties, advances and takes out the machine gun. Barker is shot at by a sniper but is able to spray the tree with his M-16, killing the sniper but is then killed by another sniper. Nagy, Gilbert, and Barker, become the 28th, 29th, and 30th to die.

12:05 hours: 2nd platoon's, Astor Caudill is attacked by two VC. He kills the two VC but is shot in both legs and sides. Caudill crawls away in the woods and someone has thrown a smoke grenade. The VC gets a fix on the position, attack and shoot Caudill twice in the head, leaving him for dead.

However, Caudill is still alive and playing dead. As Caudill is laying on the ground, another VC comes up and hits him on the top of the head, near his ear. The top part of his left ear is blown away and he loses hearing in that ear.

The VC fires another round under Caudill's jaw and leaves thinking he is dead. He has been shot twelve times but is still alive. Others from 2nd platoon find him and take him back to the NDP. [43]

Dwayne Byrd and the 2nd platoon engage the VC. Edward Vercoe, Byrd's RTO, sees a squad of VC ready to set up a machine gun. Byrd and Vercoe take out the squad of VC. A sniper in the tree shoots Vercoe in the back of the head. Then shoots out Vercoe's left kneecap and left elbow.

Griego and Domoneck are wounded. John Fowler is next to the machine gun crew of Fuqua, Crutcher, and Miller. Fuqua, next to John Fowler, is shot in the shoulder. The upper part of his right side is gone and is bleeding to death. Fuqua goes into shock and becomes the 31st to die.

Michael Miller and Joe Crutcher are returning fire, and both are killed. The point man, Donald Adkins, is killed. The three become the 32nd, 33rd, and 34th to die.

---

43   Fred Kirkpatrick interview of Astor Caudill on March 17, 2004

Fowler is near a tree and a VC sniper shoots the sight off his rifle but missed hitting Fowler. His legs are trembling. He wants to move but fear won't let him. Fowler is starting to have a mental breakdown. [44]

Melesso Garcia sees the VC in a tree and kills him. Mike Troyer comes under fire and ducks for cover behind an anthill that is shared by private Colonel Fett. Thomas Wagner, Troyer's squad leader, is about 10 meters away behind a tree. Wagner is slightly wounded.

Fett takes a bullet in the shoulder from a VC in a tree. The bullet comes out of Fett's neck. Troyer gets to his knees, rips Fett's shirt open, puts Fett's first aid patch on him.

Troyer is Yelling, "Medic." Gomez, the 2nd platoon medic, appears and pushes Troyer down and says, "You damn fool. What are you trying to do, get killed?" Gomez is able to stop the bleeding and patches Fett up.

Troyer sees Melesso Garcia, behind an anthill, gesturing, trying to say something. Garcia pushes his body up with one hand, and he's hit. He's screaming, "Doc. Hit." Troyer sees this look of horror on his face. He's spitting blood out and is trying to speak but can't. Gomez jumps and runs to the anthill to help Garcia, but he is dead, the 35th to die.

Tom Colburn, behind another anthill, is scared shitless. One of Colburn's buddies, who was in the sunlight, is hit by a sniper. He is Yelling," Colburn. Colburn." He's hit a 2nd time. Each time he asks for help, he's hit, six times in total before he dies. Colburn's whole body is trembling. He wants to help but knows he'll be killed if he moves into the sunlight.

Troyer helps Fett out of the anthill, and they move to the left rear of the Battalion CP. They come across Jimmy Scott who yells to them, "Help me. I'm hit in the back, and I can't walk."

---

44   Fred Kirkpatrick interview of John Fowler on February 28, 2004

Schroder nearby, says to Troyer, "I'm going to find out from somebody which way is out of here." Welch is yelling at them, "Go Back 360." Troyer gets his compass out. Alves runs up screaming, "Troyer. Troyer. Which way is out. You've got a compass, what's the azimuth?" Troyer says, "It's a 360." and points in that direction. [45]

12:10 hours: 1st platoon's, 2nd Lt. Luberta and his RTO Theodore Thomas, are hit and killed. Staff Sgt. Luther Smith is hit by a rocket grenade that blows off much of his leg. Sena crawls over to Smith, stops the bleeding with his first aid kit and gives Smith a cigarette. Smith dies a few minutes later. [46]

The three become the 36th, 37th, and 38th to die.

Sena is hugging the ground and lifts his rifle up and a VC shot knocks out half of his wrist. Sena takes dirt and puts it into his wound and continues to fire. Joe Moultrie, 1st platoon medic, tries to help Sena but is killed by a sniper and becomes the 39th to die.

Daniel Sikorski's six-man 2nd squad moves up to help. They come under withering fire from small arms fire, claymore mines, automatic weapons, and machine gun fire. Jackie Bolen, the point man, is killed along with the rest of the squad of Stephen Ostroff, Edward Dye, Melvin Cook, and Jackie Shubert. Sikorski remains in the open to deploy his men and is returning fire when he is mortally wounded.

The six become the 40th, 41st, 42nd, 43rd, 44th, and 45th to die.

1st squad of the 1st platoon moves forward to help and comes under intense fire. Ralph Gilliam, Edwin Felton, Robert Jensen, and Isaiah McCoy are all wounded.

Lester Dewey's 3rd squad comes under fire. Greg Landon, facing west, in the prone position, is trying to unjam Dewey's rifle that has clogged up with blood. Landon is hit on the back from the south. Landon takes his radio off to see how bad he's hit. It looks bad but isn't bad.

---

45   Captain Cash interview of John Troyer on October 22, 1967

46   David Maraniss, They Marched into Sunlight, page 271

Reynolds Lonefight is trying to get back to his 3rd squad but is pinned down by automatic fire on the right flank. He is able to move to the left flank where there is no fire and sees his wounded buddy, Landon. He bandages him up and drags him to a safe area. Lonefight is now moving on the right flank when a claymore goes off. Lonefight is hit with shrapnel in the wrist, hip, and leg.

Lester Dewey is behind a tree and can hear the bullets hit the dirt as they go over him. They make a whistling sound. Dewey is returning fire at a machine gun in front of him and takes that gun out. Dewey is now yelling, "I'm hit, I'm hit." [47]

Reynolds Lonefight braves the intense hostile fire as he rushes forward to provide covering fire for the evacuation of the wounded. The machine gun crew of Earl Hayes and Doug Cron are laying down a tremendous base of machine gun fire on the VC.

Cron is hit over and over in the hand. A total of nine separate times.

Paul Giannico from the Lucky Platoon, is next to his buddy, Roy Stephens who is hit in the leg by a claymore mine. Stephens yells, "It hurts like hell."Giannico helps Stephens to his feet, and he puts his arm around his neck.

12:15 hours: Raymond Phillips, RTO for 1st Sgt Barrow, during the first firefight, got separated from Barrow and winds up near the vicinity of the anthill where LTC Allen and his command group is located. Phillips, who was wounded early on and unable to move, has been watching the area near the command group. During a lull in the fighting, Phillips gets behind another anthill.

The VC now have zeroed in on the command area.

Hundreds of VC have them surrounded. Bodies are hit over and over. They are bouncing up and down as the rounds hit them. There are no safe spots inside the CP perimeter. [48]

---

47   Fred Kirkpatrick interview of Lester Dewey on February 13, 2004

48   SP4 Williams interview of 1SG Clarence Barrow on October 22, 1967

Inside the perimeter, Welch is talking with Captain Blackwell. As Welch is bending over him, Blackwell says something, and Welch reaches over to his side. As soon as Welch moves, the VC fire on Blackwell. They keep firing at Blackwell, while they ignore Welch, a total of twenty-five rounds into his chest. [49]

Captain Blackwell is lying on the grass, badly wounded, near death. He's moaning in pain. There is blood all over the ground. He's been shot in the groin, legs, and chest. He is crying, "Someone please help me. I'm bleeding. I'm losing a lot of blood." [50] Death finally comes to Captain Blackwell. The 46th to die.

The VC are shooting at everyone inside the perimeter. Sergeant Major Dowling is hit in the head, the legs, and arms. Blood is gushing out. He's screaming in pain as he becomes the 47th to die. Medic Archie Porter is hit in the head, chest, and legs and is shaking violently.

Porter Dies on October 21, to become the 58th killed.

Allen, covered in blood, tells Welch to pull everyone out back north to the NDP. Welch has Lovato, the senior medic, help patch up Allen. A machine gun opens up on Lovato. He is hit multiple times and becomes the 48th to die.

A . 50 caliber machine gun is pounding at the battalion area from the east. A rocket propelled grenade explodes near the battalion area, sending black smoke up in the air. Pieces of bodies are landing in different places.

Part of the blast strikes Allen in the face. Allen's RTO, Pasquale Tizzio is killed. Tizzio is sprawled on the ground face down, part of his shoulder ripped off. Allen trying to get the radio off Tizzio, to call in more artillery fire, is wounded by VC fire that kills Gilbertson, Plier, and Randall. RTO James Larson is killed.

The five become the 49th, 50th, 51st, 52nd, and 53rd to die.

---

49   SP4 Williams interview of LT Clark Welch on October 20, 1967

50   Captain Cash interview of Roy Stephens and Paul Giannico on October 21, 1967

Stroup crawls about 50 yards and reaches Allen who is still conscious. His glasses are off, and blood is running down his face. Allen says to Stroup, "Who's in charge here?" Stoup says, "I am." "What do you intend to do?" Stroup says, "I'm getting as many people as I can and we're leaving." George Smith, 3rd platoon Sgt, has joined them. A sniper shoots Stoup's compass out of his hand giving him a slight hand wound.

12:20 hours: Smith is trying to get the radio off Tizzio and a bullet glance off Allen's helmet and hits George Smith. Phillips, who has crawled over, sees bullet holes in Allen's head. One of Allen's eyes is shot out. He dies a few seconds later.

All nine from the Battalion group are now dead. Allen is the 54th soldier to die from the Battalion.

Stoup is yelling, "Let's get the hell out of here." Stoup leaves with George Smith, Doc Adams, Raymond Phillips, David Laub, and Welch. His arm is hanging down, blood is coming out. He is very weak and near death.

Welch gives Stoup a compass and says, "Lieutenant Stroup, please get my company out of here." [51] Paul Scott and Stroup help to carry Welch. Stoup gives the compass to Laub and says, "Go back 360 now." Laub heads towards a clearing that is about 30 yards wide.

Peter Miller reaches the Battalion area a few minutes later and sees Schroder on his knees praying. Miller is yelling, "Let's get going." Miller crawls away and Schroder follows.

McMeel crawls and finds Griego on the ground, motionless but still breathing. McMeel says to Griego, "Come on, we're getting out of here." They crawl out together. [52]

---

51   Captain Cash interview of David Stroup on October 22, 1967

52   David Maraniss, They Marched into Sunlight, pages 279-281

Schroder, with severe leg wounds, crawls behind the command group. Schroder's legs are shot over and over. He wants to crawl away but can't move. He is unable to run and crying out in pain. A VC appears and shoots him in the heart, killing him. He becomes the 55th to die.

Troyer is moving towards the NDP with Fett and Jimmy Scott. They are joined by Doc Adams, 3rd platoon medic, who is preaching, "Stand up with me. God is with us. We'll make it." Doc Adams, hit it the right arm, right elbow, and left shoulder, is trying to help them but can't do much. Adams is making Jimmy Scott repeat, "He maketh me to lie down in green pastures. He leadeth me beside the still water." [53]

Valdez and his group of about 25 have decided to withdraw back to the NDP. Arias is leading them out. Many of the men are wounded. They have been stumbling through the jungle, dodging friendly artillery fire and VC fire. As Valdez reaches the clearing near the NDP, he spots Lt. Erwin from the Recon platoon and comes over to Erwin. Valdez says, "It's a massacre, Sir." [54]

13:00 hours: Major Holleder, Brigade S3, has arrived on the NDP and says to Lt Erwin, "We have to get in there and help them, they are in trouble and need help."

The Major, on a dead run through tall grass and knew-deep water, moves about 350-400 meters. A single shot from a VC sniper in a tree mortally wounds Holleder.

Major Holleder, the 156th man to join the fight, becomes the 56th of fifty-nine to die from the Battle of Ong Thanh.

16:30 hours: PSG George Smith leads a group of sixty back to the Battalion CP area. They reach the area of the anthill and find

---

53   Captain Cash interview of John Troyer on October 22, 1967

54   David Maraniss, They Marched into Sunlight, page 291

nearly twenty-five died around Allen. They find six dead VC bodies inside the Battalion CP and soldiers Clarence Barrow who is badly wounded, and RTO, Joe Booker, in shock, pale, unresponsive, and incoherent with a major abdominal wound, but still alive. [55]

Booker becomes the 57th to die on October 18. Willie C. Johnson, my friend and mentor, dies on November 9th, to become the 59th to die.

Oct 8, 1967 - Team of reporters waiting as we go out on mission deemed to be HOT

55   Dave Berry - Joe Booker - Died of Wounds 18 Oct 67, www. pbase. com/d_ berry/image/151208302

Fred Kirkpatrick, April 1967, sign at front of LaiKhe

Oct 8, 1967 – Delta company soldiers waiting to go out on a mission.

Fred Kirkpatrick, April 1967 with M-79

Wilbert Peters on far left, killed Feb 21, 1968, from Artillery rocket mortar as he lay sleeping in bed. Fred Kirkpatrick walking alongside him.

Vietnamese Village 1967

Huey Helicopters flying in format transporting soldiers to a mission.

Fred Kirkpatrick in front. Gary Lincoln from Ohio, KIA 10/17/67 in the background.

Fred Kirkpatrick, Nov 1967, after he was promoted to Sgt E-5.

Huey Helicopter with no doors to save weight and make it easier to get in and out.

Mess hall at LaiKhe, Vietnam 1967

Kenneth Wilson carrying M60 machine gun. Killed in action
10/17/67

Miss South Carolina 1966, Barbara Harris, August 1967, shaking
hands with Richard Jones, KIA - 10/17/67

Bob Hope, Christmas 1967, LaiKhe, Vietnam

Raquel Welch, Christmas 1967, on stage at LaiKhe, Vietnam

Fred Kirkpatrick, Oct 1967, in front holding compass. Sitting next to him is Gary Lincoln from Ohio. KIA 10/17/67

Rachel Welch, Christmas 1967

CHAPTER **6**

The Return from Japan

(October 21, 1967 - January 9, 1968)

USO Club, Tokyo, Japan – October 21, 1967: Roy Key and I have left the Club Bohemian, heading to the USO club in downtown Tokyo to pick up the day's edition of "Stars & Stripes" to see what is going on in Vietnam. When we get to the club, I sign the guest book and pick up the newspaper. The front headline reads,

"103 Reds Killed in Triple attack on US Battalion."

I keep reading about the eight-hour battle in which fifty-six US soldiers are killed and sixty-three are wounded. At first I didn't get the connection:

"Among the dead were Lt. Col Terry Allen Jr. of the 1st Infantry, 28th Infantry."

Then the connection becomes painfully clear. I yell to Key, "Roy come here." He comes over and I show him the paper. Roy reads the story and is as shocked as I am. We start thinking, Oh My God They got wiped out, since we thought there were only about 200 men in two companies.

I'm very agitated and say to Roy, "That fuckin Allen, He got them all killed. They got wiped out."

I'm talking to myself, "I never dreamed something like this could ever happen. I feel sick since I don't know who is alive and who is dead."

LATER THAT NIGHT, me and my Japanese girlfriend, Keiko, are on our last date before I leave the next morning. She and I met during my first R & R in June to Japan. Keiko takes me to a local market so that we can eat.

I tell her, " I'm not hungry." She can see that I'm not my old friendly and fun self and tries to get me to open up.

"Freddy, what's wrong? You seem very upset. Did I do something wrong?"

"You haven't done anything wrong. Thinking of going back to Vietnam tomorrow has me on edge."

As we are walking along, some Japanese man walks by and accidentally bumps into me. I'm yelling at him, "What the fucks your problem asshole." The man makes a move towards me, and I cock my fist, about to strike. From out of nowhere, Keiko jumps in front of us and raises her hand and stops my fist. Keiko says something to the man, and he leaves. I'm amused, thinking that Keiko must know karate to have stopped my motion so quickly.

A burning rage and hatred is eating up my insides. I'm sick to my stomach and can't wait to get back to Vietnam to find out who is alive.

LONG BINH, VIETNAM – OCTOBER 23, 1967 – AFTERNOON: William Crosby, from Charlie Company, is waiting at the airport for the plane that's carrying those returning from R & R to land. Crosby says to himself, "I hope it's not true. It can't be true." Crosby, from Georgia, and I took basic training at Fort Benning, GA in August 1966. We also served together in Charlie company when we both arrived in Vietnam. We have become very close friends.

Crosby has the task of making sure those who were on R & R are accounted for. The plane lands and Black Lions are getting off. Key, Hammonds, and I are all together.

I see Crosby and go up to my old friend. "Hey Crosby, what are you doing here?"

He says, "I'm here to make sure everyone who was supposed to be on R & R actually was."

Tears start to form in Crosby's eyes. I say, "What's wrong with you?"

"I heard you were killed on October 17 and I wanted to make sure it wasn't true."

"Well buddy, it is not true. I'm here. We are going to the hospital to visit the guys." We all leave for the Ninety-third Evacuation Hospital in LaiKhe.

A few minutes later, we all arrive at the hospital. My eyes light up as I think I see Megiveron with a neck brace on. I rush to talk with him. But my happiness quickly turns to sadness.

It's Griego, Roy's friend and he says, "Megiveron was killed on October 17." Roy stops to talk with his friend Griego.

I spot my friend, Willie C. Johnson from Charlie Company. He is alive, but in critical condition. I'm shocked at the site of Johnson. He's wrapped in a blanket, and it looks like some part of his body is missing. His eyes are as yellow as mustard. Johnson underwent removal of part of a bleeding liver.

Johnson sees me and starts talking to me. "I'm glad you weren't their Kirk. It was horrible. They were everywhere." I'm talking to the nurse. "Is he going to make it?" The Nurse shakes her head no, "He's been shot over 100 times. His liver is shot. It's only a matter of time."

An hour later, I'm on my way back to the Delta company area. It's been less than two weeks and the company is completely different. Half of the company I knew is gone. Gone is our company commander Clark Welch and 1st Sgt. Barrow. Both badly wounded and in a hospital in Japan.

Captain Grosso is now the company commander. Sgt Smith, who came to Delta on October 14, is now the 1st Sgt. Only 2nd Lt. Stroup & David Laub, from 3rd platoon, remain as the only combination of Platoon Leader and Platoon Leader RTO in the company. The 1st, 2nd, and 3rd platoons are completely different. They are replaced by many new guys called "the replacements."

Bringing in Replacements is a rare event since they come to replace only when many are killed or wounded in one event.

Only Reynolds Lonefight remains from my squad. Lincoln, Megiveron, Jones, Reece, Schroder, and Wilson are all dead. Hodges and McMeel are badly wounded, recovering in Japan, and will not return to Vietnam.

I ask Reynolds, "What about Gerald Thompson." He says, "Gerald left the field on October 16 with infections in both feet. Both of his feet were swollen to twice their size and he could not even put his socks on. Some General asked Gerald to help identify the bodies. Gerald identifies Col. Allen and Luther Smith by his big gold ring on his finger since most of his head and lips were gone.

Gerald also identified Lincoln, Megiveron, and Reece. It made Gerald sick to his stomach, and I think the General helped get him off the field. He's now the mail clerk for Delta company."

I'm now the 3rd platoon, 3rd squad leader.

I walk over to 1st Sgt Smith and say, "I want to see if I can get my compass back." He points to a huge pile of equipment that was brought back from the battle. I look through the equipment, find a compass that has blood all over it, clean the blood off and take the compass.

The Battle of Loc Ninh - October 29 to November 3, 1967: The first engagement begins at 0100 hours on October 29, 1967. Elements of the 273d VC Regiment attack the village of Loc Ninh and overran portions of the perimeter and enter the village. Then they attack our positions at the compound at the end of the airport runway. The next morning on October 30, Charlie company, teamed up with CIDG and ARVN forces to retake the village from the VC. As a result of this engagement, 92 VC are killed.

The 3rd day of the battle, October 31, the 2nd Battalion, 28th Infantry, began firing harassment and interdiction mortar fire. An hour later, the VC attack the Black Lions NDP with mortars, small arms fire, and RPG's. Our battalion responded with helicopter gunships, artillery, and airstrikes on the VC.

0515 hours: Wave after wave of VC come storming across the airfield. They come out of the woods by the hundreds in a suicide charge. The strong smell of marijuana is present. They are charging and shooting at our artillery guns. The 2/28th unleashes all their firepower of the attached artillery battery on the charging enemy. Artillery guns are lowered and aimed right at the charging Viet Cong. Our artillery guns fire canister rounds at almost point-blank range.

The results are deadly. The trees are split into two. The VC suffers the same fate. Razor sharp canister rounds by the thousands are ripping into the bodies of the VC. Body parts are flying everywhere. Arms are detached from their shoulders. Heads are removed from bodies. Pieces of flesh are hurtled into trees.

Airstrikes are also placed on the airstrip. This repelled the insurgent's fanatical attack. The battle rages all day. At 1700 hours, contact is broken.

This is considered one of the greatest battles of the Vietnam War. It was reported that we had killed over 1,000 Viet Cong, while only losing ten men.

Charlie company is told they will be going back to LaiKhe. My company will replace them on November 1. Delta 2/28 lands at the airstrip where the three-day battle had ended. This is a remote outpost, about 40 miles north of LaiKhe.

I walk around the area with others and see that the trees are split into two. There is a huge trench dug to bury the dead VC. I see hundreds of dead VC in pieces with arms detached from their shoulders. Heads are removed from bodies and pieces of flesh can be found in the trees. These dead VCs looked much darker than other VC I had seen before. I'm thinking maybe they are not Vietnamese, maybe Chinese.

Earlier in the afternoon, a Chinook brings in extra ammo for us. The 1st Infantry Division is expecting another attack like on day three since they did the same "trick" as before. They take out one Infantry company, Charlie company, and one battery of artillery. They know the VC are watching our every move. We are expecting another human-wave attack and I'm looking forward to killing as many VC as I can.

On my right, is the Special Forces/Civilian Defense Group (CIDG) compound. The Special Forces compound is next to the airstrip. The 2/28th perimeter is at the end of the airstrip. My bunker is the lead bunker. The VC last time attacked from that position.

I prepare to do battle that night and load up on all the ammo and firepower I can. The Chinook has brought in a 50-caliber machine gun with lots of ammo that I take to my bunker. I have my M-16 rifle, 20 claymore mines in front of my position, 40-50 LAW's, 100 or more grenades, and thousands of rounds of ammo. I don't plan to go quietly, and I will kill as many VC as I can.

Around midnight, I'm telling the new guy's war stories about mortar rounds. How you can tell the different rounds by the sounds they make. Almost as soon as the words are out of my mouth,

pop, pop, pop - can be heard

I hear the familiar sounds of 60mm fire. I yell "Incoming", grab one of the new guys and push him into the bunker. I have the others follow us into the bunker.

Within seconds, we are hit with incoming 60mm mortar rounds. The sky is lit from overhead as our planes are dropping "light" for us to see. We wait for the great battle. I let loose with a short burst from my 50-caliber machine gun to "induce" Charlie to attack me. This sure wake everyone up. My platoon leader, 2nd Lt. Stroup, yells at me, "Stop Shooting." I stop and wait for the attack. Minutes pass that seems like years. Charlie doesn't show.

Later that night, around 2am, we can feel the ground shaking, like a small earthquake below us. It's our B-52's dropping tons of bombs. They are about 35-40 miles away and are dropping bombs from an altitude so high the VC are unaware of the attack until the jungle around them starts shaking.

The next night, I take my squad out for an ambush patrol and let one of the C Packet guys, Gilbert Pizano, take point. However, I stay very close to him. The "Chief" is next to me at all times. The rest of the squad are "the replacements" with less than one month in country.

We setup about 700-800 meters from our NDP. Around 2am, I hear movement in front of me. I hear VC talking. They are getting closer, no more than ten yards away. I'm having trouble breathing as I fight to remain calm. I check on the rest of my squad and they are all sleeping. I try to wake up the machine gunner and the others, but to no avail, they are all in a deep sleep.

I have the radio in my hand, signaling back at the NDP that I have movement and wait to spring the ambush. The voices are almost on top of us. I whisper to the Chief, "Get ready, it will just be the two of us."

If I pull this ambush off and kill a few VC, I will be decorated for heroism. I'm ready to kill these little bastards.

The VC must have heard us and are now moving away from us. I decide to call in a "fire mission" and fire a few mortar rounds in front of us. The first round appears to be too close. I adjust it and have a few mortars fire in front of me. After that, the long sleepless night finally ends without any other incident. When we get back to the NDP, the new company commander starts giving me shit.

"So where are the dead bodies?" I just walk past him.

November 3: We are back at LaiKhe. By the middle of December, I am no longer in the field. My last two weeks are spent back at LaiKhe, processing out of Vietnam.

December 26, 1967: Bob Hope comes to LaiKhe with his Christmas show, but I don't get to see the show. I'm in a forty-foot tower, part of those who are guarding the show. General Hay, commander of the 1st Infantry Division, greets Bob Hope and points out to the huge crowd of soldiers. The General says, "These war-weary veterans have been in eight major conflicts in 1967." The only problem with that was that only a handful in the audience had ever saw combat in 1967. Many of them are the fat-cat non-combat veterans.

January 1, 1968: Early morning, around 3am, LaiKhe comes under a heavy rocket attack. I'm listening on the radio and hear,

"We Are Being Overrun."

It is a sick feeling to hear this with very few infantrymen back at LaiKhe to help us. This turns out to be a false alarm because new troops on the front lines panicked.

January 3, 1967: I'm getting ready to head out of LaiKhe to start processing out of country and stop to say goodbye to the guys. As usually, Reynolds is not around, he's at the village with his pregnant girlfriend. I spot Marino and stop to talk with him.

Marino was at the battle on October 17 and survived but is scared for his life.

Marino says to me, " I'm not going out in the field again."

I said, "How are you going to do that, you still have three months left on your tour."

Marino flashes a smile and points a finger across his teeth. "See these."

I said, "So what."

Marino says, I'm going to have each one pulled one at a time and that should take nearly three months."

I laugh, "Great plan buddy. How will I know it works."

Marino laughs and says, "Write me when you get back to the states and I'll let you know how the plan works."

I said, "OK, I'll write you when I get back."

Marino says, "I don't believe you. I want you to promise me you will write me."

I say, "I promise you and hope to see you in Ohio soon."

A few minutes later, Peters comes up to me and says, "Can I have ye bed Kirk since I see y'all are fixing to leave. Finger y'all don't need it no more."

Peters and I have become close friends. I say to him, "Sure Peters, I hope the bed brings you good luck."

Peters responds back, "Yeah, y'all not be knee den it no more. You might ought to think about visiting me and my kinfolks in Mo-bee. My mama can cook you up some good old Southern cooking for y'all."

I say, "Thanks, Peters, that sounds really good. I'll be sure to visit you in Mobile, Alabama." Peters has a broad smile on his face as he lays on his new bed.

At the processing center, they try to get me to sign up to stay three more months in Vietnam. If I agreed to stay in Vietnam till the end of March 1968, they will waive the remain eight months of duty I would have to do state side. I decline the offer thinking I've already pushed my luck too far.

January 9, 1968: I'm on a plane at Cam Rahn Bay bound for the states. I can now continue with the good life I left behind two years ago.

CHAPTER 7

That's Impossible

(January 1968 - August 1968)

The commercial jet aircraft is packed with military personnel as it lifts off the ground in Vietnam bound for the United States. We all hold our breaths collectively until we are out of range from enemy fire. When the plane reaches cruising attitude at about 30,000 feet, everyone on board erupts into cheers.

My one-year nightmare is over. I can now return to my normal life:

College students were protesting the use of Napalm bombs on the Vietnamese people, but silent on the use of Agent Orange against the Vietnamese people and American soldiers; **"Perhaps the most toxic molecule ever synthesized by man",** *linked to at least 15 classes of cancer and other medical conditions and several birth defects.* [56]

The North Vietnamese Army and Viet Cong were supported by China and the Soviet Union. Ships transporting arms and supplies, necessary for North Vietnam's war effort, landed unopposed at Haiphong. Port areas were off limits from attacks where the Soviet Union was providing

---

56   Agent Orange, www. agentorangerecord. com/home

sophisticated weapons like the SA2, SA3, missiles, MIG 19s, large-caliber rockets and artillery, and PT-76 tanks to the North. American pilots were not allowed to drop bombs around Hanoi and Haiphong for fear that China or the Soviet Union, would intervene militarily.

The medal awarding process, where clerks and officers, with the stoke of a pen, could issue medals to themselves and their friends. Many of them had never been in the field. One of the most blatant examples was Major General Hay who issued himself a Silver Star for a battle that he was not even a part of. [57]

*Some Grave Registration (**Robbers**) personnel, whose main function was to process dead American soldiers, would steal items and money off the dead bodies as they processed them.* [58]

After leaving Vietnam, I was flown into a military station in Oakland, California, to be processed out of my duty in Vietnam and into my next assignment. The plane ride from California to Cleveland was something of a fog. It was like being released from a ten-year prison sentence; I wore my dress blue army uniform with patches and medals. I had a very deep suntan that marked me as a returning combat soldier. No one on the way spoke to me or asked me any questions.

At Cleveland Hopkins Airport, there was no one to greet me. I called my mother to see if anyone was going to pick me up. There was no answer, so I decided to take a taxicab home. As I head out to hail a taxicab, I encounter a big crowd of antiwar protesters with various signs: *Napalm Kills Vietnamese Children, Baby Killers, Losers.* Some are spitting on the ground in front of us. In the crowd are several veterans with signs, *Vietnam Veterans are Losers.* Others are chatting, *Baby Killers.*

While in Vietnam, it was very demoralizing to read about war protestors at college campuses doing sit-ins, marches, and demonstrations,

---

57   Did U. S. military really earn all their medals, John T. Reed, www. johnreed. com/militarymedals. html

58   Notes given to me from Fred Mager who was weapons platoon leader for 2/28th Delta in 1967.

and destroying property. The worst was the full-scale riot at the pentagon on October 21, 1967. Around 35,000 protestors scaled walls and forced their way into the pentagon. Deputy Marshalls and soldiers were taunted and assaulted with vegetables, rocks, and bottles. [59],

I am humiliated and ashamed and do not want anyone to know I am a Vietnam veteran. I feel like a freak and want to get home and get out of my uniform. As soon as I got home, I get out of my uniform and put everything from my time in Vietnam in the attic to quickly forget about Vietnam and move on with my life.

A week later, I take a greyhound bus to my post at Fort Knox, Kentucky. It was a completely different world to me. I am a young twenty-one-year-old buck sergeant with long hair and no longer used to following the bullshit state-side Army rules.

The first week was a temporary location. Here all returning Veterans are processed in until their permanent duty station is available. During that time, we were under the control of a sick sadistic power-hungry Spec 4 by the name of Damien Lizard.

He would bully everyone, especially those back from Vietnam who had make the rank of Sergeant while in combat. In fact, most of the lifers who had been in the Army over ten years, where rank to Sergeant usually took fifteen years, did not like us "instant NCO's." In combat you could become an instant non-com officer (NCO), as those who had the various ranks of Sergeant were known, in less than one year. They bullied us because they knew they could. Most coming back from the war had a short period of time to serve and did not want to create waves and get busted down a rank.

The day before I was to leave for my permanent assignment, the Lizard was being a prick to my friend from Vietnam. Finally, I had

---

59   Pentagon Riot of October 21, 1967 - https://www. globalsecurity. org/military/ops/pentagon-1967. htm

enough and snapped. Within a few seconds, my 5' 6", 145lb frame was in the face of the 6' 2", 215 lb. Damien Lizard. The rage within me and what came out surprised me. A fury of hate came spilling out as I stood up to this bully.

"You piece of shit; I'm going to beat your ass. Let us go into the bathroom and settle this now."

I clinched both my fists in a ball. I could feel my heart beating faster and faster. I thought my heart might explode. the Lizard kept looking away from me knowing that one wrong move or look would further enrage me. As all cowards do, he left to tell his supervisors.

As he left, I yelled, "You fucking coward." I left after calming down. the Lizard came back with a Sergeant that had a higher rank then me. To cover his fear, he said some Sergeant, who outranked him, threatened him, and he could not say anything. I wonder if he mentioned to that Sergeant that I "offered" him a chance to settle things in the bathroom where I would remove my "stripes". The Army fixed the problem by promoting the Lizard to a buck Sergeant.

For the next few weeks, I am on base with no nothing to do, as I wait for a permanent assignment. For over a week, I am sleeping 12-15 hours a day, yet wake up exhausted. I have extraordinarily little energy and no desire to do anything. The last five days, I struggle to sleep. I fear for my life. I struggle to stay awake but finally exhaustion overtakes me, and I drift into sleep. But any little noise, especially loud noises, startles me out of even the deepest sleep. The nightmares about death are scary and feel like they are real, but I cannot be sure that they are:

It is a beautiful summer day, and I am walking in an open field of lush grass surrounded by grooves of trees. Beyond the open field, maybe 1-2 miles away, is a valley with a stream flowing through it. The area is peaceful and quiet, unspoiled by human contact.

As I walk further along, I see in the distance, near the valley, dark shapes, and outlines of something that looks human. When I am within 200 yards, I can make out the form of five white males. They appear to be waving as I get closer.

When I get within 100 yards, I can see they are older teenagers. One is tall and lanky with blond hair. Another, the shortest of the group, has flaming red hair. A third one is tall and stocky built like John Wayne. A fourth, around 5' 9", has blond hair with a cool smile like Paul Newman. The last one has dark brown hair and looks something like James Dean.

Not sure why, but I think they look familiar, and walk faster to get a better look. In an instant, the quiet of the open field turns violent. There are sounds of multiple guns shoots, followed by screams of horror.

I run to get closer but am stopped in my tracks when I'm within 50 yards. I hit some invisible fence that prevents me from getting closer.

The tall lanky one is hit in the throat from a bullet and is spitting out blood. He is unable to move or talk.

The redhead is hit in both legs and arms. Another round hits him in the head and his head exploded.

Bullets are hitting all around the cool smile guy. He gets up to sprint for cover and is shot in the back, flipping him over.

The linebacker is running for cover. I see blood running down from a stump where his right hand has been blown off.

The guy with the dark brown hair, is hit in the groin, chest, and right leg. He is bleeding badly.

I bolt up in bed, waking up from another nightmare I am experiencing.

After a few weeks, the company commander comes to me and said he has my new position. I am to be a "Commander-of-Relief" at a mountain post about ten miles from the main post. I will have five men under me and two Army jeeps. Each of my men will have twelve-gauge shotguns. I will have a . 45 caliber pistol. I will be under only two people on the post, regardless of rank, my company commander, and the post commander.

The area is very remote and restricted. Military Police patrol the road leading up to the mountain post. Anyone entering the gate must show an ID during the day. During the day, our orders are to give one warning shot to anyone not following orders. The next shot will be "shoot to kill."At night, the orders are different. No one is allowed to enter during the night after 6PM and the gate is closed. There are no warning shots. It is only "shoot to kill."

We were all combat Vietnam Veterans. All soldiers on post fear us. Any one of us would be happy to comply with those orders. We had so much security on the mountain top because some of the underground bunkers contained some especially important weapons.

During our nine-day assignment, we work three days from 4 AM-12 Noon; followed by three days from Noon to 8PM; finally, 8PM to 4AM. The first two shifts are the busy ones because troops are inside the area and went back and forth. They are making ammo for the exotic weapons for those guarding our gold supply.

My favorite shift is the one from 8PM to 4AM. During that time, the gate is locked, and no one is allowed in or out of after 6PM. A few times someone tried to challenge our authority and was nearly killed.

One of my guys had to put a major in the pushup position for several hours. The major tried to challenge his authority. He held a shotgun to his head and there was fear for his life. This caused a big stir among the state side people. I had a problem with a Captain who in the morning walked past me without showing his ID. I fired a warning shot over his head and yelled, "Get back here and show me your ID or the next round will be in your head." He quickly came back.

During the next month, I learn how to play pinochle, drink, and even had time to kill a fox. I already have two of the three skills: Drinking and killing. Pinochle is a newly acquired skill.

Today I had to kill a fox on our compound. It was feared the fox might be rabid because it was acting aggressively and was not afraid of people. It became my responsibility to shoot and kill it with my . 45 caliber pistol. That turned out to not be such an easy task.

I am in the passenger seat as Roger, and I approach the running fox. I am about twenty feet away and first my first round, but I miss. I yell to Roger, "Get closer, point-blank range."

"Point blank" in this case would be four or five feet.

I am on the side of the fox as he tries to run away. My second round blows off his back leg. The bone is almost certainly smashed.

The fox is moving at a slower pace now. With the third round, I hit him in the middle of his body and the impact flips him over, but he keeps moving.

The exit wound is almost always bigger than the entry wound. The round mushrooms, spreading the energy through the target. The fox will not survive. He will die from blood loss or an infection from the wound.

Shot placement is the big key. If you do not hit a vital structure, the victim may not be stopped right away. The physical incapacitation did not damage the critical structure yet. But this fox has the psychological will to live. He refuses to give up and die.

I must finish the job. I keep firing at the fox till I am out of rounds. This was no longer a battle with just a fox, it was me flipped out and on a flashback to Vietnam. I am scared for my life.

It was a bloody mess when the MPs took the fox away. They were upset that I had used all the rounds from my weapon. I told them it would not stop and kept moving and I had to make sure it was dead.

On occasions I was exposed to the chickenshit stateside army life. One day I was walking back to my barracks and had my hat off. Suddenly some insane Sergeant Major is in my face screaming at me. "Why are you not wearing a hat? Your hair is too long, get it cut."

He is the biggest and meanest guy on earth, an Army lifer with stripes that went all the way up and down both of his arms. He looks into my eyes with his ice blue eyes that could kill a normal person, and said, "You don't give a shit do you." I thought, wow, this lunatic knows me, but didn't think he was kidding, so I didn't reply. He then walked off in a big cloud of windbag smoke.

A few days later, as I was reporting into the command center, one of the lifer Sergeants told me that the Sergeant Major had recommended an article 15 for me. He said I was to be busted down one rank, from Sergeant to Corporal. The Sergeant went on to say, "I think you're the best-looking guy I've ever seen" and that he threw those orders away. I thanked him and thought how lucky for me that this Sergeant liked me. It was kind of funny to think this big tough Sergeant Major was upstaged by a man he probably hated more than me.

About the middle of February 1968, I kept my promise to Harry Marino and wrote him in Vietnam. Near the end of February, I received a letter from him. He said that on February 21, 1968, LaiKhe came under a rocket/mortar attack. Wilbert Peters, sleeping in the bed that I "willed" to him, took a direct hit. His head was blown off. He was killed instantly. The only person killed. It made me sick to know that because of me, Wilbert Peters is dead.

I never wrote back.

My last day in the Army started out with me and my friend Roger going out drinking before I left in the morning to civilian life. We hit what seemed like just about every nightclub in Kentucky. I was well on my way to being totally drunk, so I decided it was time to leave. I told Roger and he said have one more drink. I really did not want any more drinks but thought one more drink could not hurt.

The last drink looked like clear alcohol in a regular size glass. Guess it was about eight ounces. I tried to swallow it whole but could not. It felt like my throat was on fire and I had to put the glass down. I asked Roger what was in that glass. He promised to tell me if I finished the drink. With great difficulty, I was able to finish the drink. Roger then told me I had just drank seven shots of 151 Rum. He thought it was funny to see me so drunk.

Less than an hour later, we are back at Roger's apartment, and I said, "I have to leave." Roger begged me not to leave. He said I was too drunk to drive. I said do not worry. I wanted to leave and that was that. I stumbled to my car, got in my car, and backed up and hit something. I pull out, in a daze. I am taking to myself:

"Why can't I feel the pain? Why Didn't I Die? I cannot stand living this way. I must die."

I pull forward and drive till I got to a major Kentucky highway. Then something must have compelled me to pull over sideways into the highway. I put the car into park, fell out, and crawl away from the car to a curb area. I am laying on a main highway in a pool of my vomit. Traffic is stopped. Flashing police lights are all around me. I want to move but cannot. I am trying to say something but cannot form the words very well. I am speaking in a slur. Two officers are looking over at me. I am laying on the curb, my white T-shirt a dirty mess, my hair filled with vomit. One officer picks me up and carries me to his police cruiser and asks me,

"Who Was Driving?" I Said, "I Was." He said, "That's Impossible."

Early the next morning, I wake up and my T-shirt is filthy black. My hair is matted with vomit. I am shocked to see I am behind bars in a jail cell. In a panic, I yell out to a nearby guard, "Did I Kill Anyone?"

Later that morning, I stood before a judge to await my sentence. And what a sight I was with my filthy white t-shirt and matted black hair full of vomit.

The Judge says to me, "Mr. Kirkpatrick what were you doing last night?"

"Your honor, I was celebrating my discharge from the Army. I've been having problems since my return from Vietnam, and I had too much to drink."

The Judge remarks, "Son, your blood alcohol was . 38, nearly five times the legal limit, sufficient enough to kill a person. When the officers found you, they believed you exhibited signs of alcohol poisoning because of your vomiting, low body temperature, confusion, and irregular breathing. You were awfully close to slipping into a coma. I think your damn lucky to be alive."

"The officers said you did not damage to anyone, or anything, and offered no resistance to arrest. I find it absurd the notion that you think you were driving. Every one of the officers believes that to be impossible. Therefore, I can only charge you with the crime of loitering. How do you plead?"

"I plead guilty your honor."

I was fined $25 dollars and released. I was incredibly lucky this was a military town.

CHAPTER 8

The Boys Are Back

(1968-1972)

> *Our military service is over. The six amigos are back home safe, but not sound.*

The buddy plan did not turn out the way Ray and John had hoped. John was assigned to Alameda Naval Station in Alameda, California, on San Francisco Bay. John trained to become an Aviation Electronics Technician to troubleshoot and repair a number of complex electronics systems. Eight months later, John extended his tour by six months to get port of duty in Japan. At this duty, he was part of a detachment, that would for six-week intervals, fly to Da Nang Air Base Vietnam, to provide ground support for naval reconnaissance electronics equipment squads:

> *Just before noon, on March 16, 1970, a four-engine U. S. Navy propeller-driven EC-121, PR-26, that had left the port of Japan, crashed at Da Nang Air Base, Vietnam. The airliner was packed with advanced electronic monitoring equipment. Most of those aboard were technicians operating the equipment. Of the thirty-one U. S. Navy personnel aboard, twenty-three did not survive. As the plane was coming in for a landing, a tar truck was crossing on the runway, the plane had to abort the landing to avoid hitting the truck. But during the pull up, the number 3 engine feathered, stalling the aircraft and it cartwheeled into a USAF hanger,*

destroying an F-4 Phantom jet fighter-bomber parked near the runway. It then hit a steel-covered aircraft revetment, bounced and broke into three pieces: The cocktail and fuselage forward of the wing, slid into a revetment wall and burned fiercely killing all 23 inside; The center section with four aboard, crashed upside down into a street and burned. The four inside survived but were gravely injured; The tail section landed on a softball field and did not burn. One man in the tail section, walked away unscathed. [60]

John was sick the day before the flight and missed death by one day. He suffers from survivor guilt and believes he did something wrong by surviving the traumatic crash on March 16, 1970.

Because Ray didn't have a high diploma, he was unqualified to train as an Aviation Electronics Technician. Ray was able to get an assignment to a Naval Base in Key West, Florida, as an Aviation Electricians Mate "A" school that would take him to Vietnam.

Earlier during basic training, while marching, he tore up his arches and went to the sick bay and some doctor told him to do certain exercises to strengthen his arches, but never told him to report back. After he completed all his training, Ray's bag was packed as he prepared for deployment on the Coral Sea aircraft carrier to Vietnam.

While waiting for deployment, Ray's wrist developed a ganglion that needed to be drained. After getting his wrist drained, he was walking out of the hospital and a doctor noticed that his legs were cracking and producing a popping sound. The doctor stopped him and said he needs to be checked. The doctor found Ray's records from basic training and the incident about arches and that a follow-up should have been performed. The doctor gave him orders to report back to the hospital to have his feet examined.

For forty-five days, three doctors perform tests on his feet as he is confined to the hospital area. After the forty-five days, Ray is ready

---

60   16 March 1970 - http://pr26-vietnam. com

to deploy with his unit to Vietnam. However, to Ray's amazement, a Petty Officer first class come up to him and hands him an honorable discharge and told him, "Your feet and legs won't hold up on board ship."

A very disappointed Ray was given a medical honorable discharge on August 1969. Even though it was not his fault, Ray feels guilty because he was the only one of us to not serve in Vietnam.

Geno and Denny should not have been out of the service until August 1969, but unusual circumstances changed that.

Geno had been stationed near the Demilitarized Zone (DMZ), with the 3rd Marine Division. He was involved in heavy combat during the Tet Offensive on January 30, 1968. And in February 1968, he was severely wounded during the Battle of Hue, one of the bloodiest and longest battles of the Vietnam War. He was shot in the leg that shattered his femur, and his leg is now held together with plates and pins, and he has a permanent limp. Geno spent nearly six months recovering in military hospitals, before getting his medical discharge on August 1968.

During Geno's recovery, he was given Opioid pain medications that helped with the pain. But after so many months of taking these painkillers, he developed a tolerance to the medications and needed an increased dosage to feel the same effect. After his recovery and release, the pain medicine was reduced.

He started feeling horrible, experiencing body aches, restlessness, and insomnia. He was depressed, sleeping either 3 hours or 15 hours per day. He was losing touch with reality as he became more violent and paranoid. The pain had increased to an almost unbearable burden. So, Geno turned to marijuana and amphetamines for relief. He found little, so he turned to heroin that gave him the relief he desperately needed. He enjoyed heroin because it sped up the perception of time and gave him the sensation of pleasure, with a warm, cozy, and relaxed feeling.

Geno is here physically but is mentally absent. He is withdrawn from the world as we used to know it. There is no happiness in him, only sadness and daily pain.

Denny, or Ace as I would call him at times, surprised me with all his problems since he was stationed at Cam Rahn Bay, one of the safest places to be in Vietnam.

The U. S. Army maintained the 6th convalescent center at Cam Rahn Bay, where wounded American soldiers were treated. This major military seaport was used for loading supplies, military equipment, and as a major naval base. It's natural inner and outer harbors formed what many believed, to be, the best and most beautiful deep-water port in the entire world. [61]

"Hey Ace, what happened over in Vietnam with you. I thought you had pretty good duty at Cam Rahn Bay." Denny said, "Yeah Fred it was great duty till about November 67. Then I got a new assignment to the 1st Logistic Division U. S. Army Mortuary at Tan Son Nhut Air Base in Saigon." I said, "No shit, I didn't know that. How was it at the morgue?"

"It was horrible. First, I worked on unloading of the green body bags of dead American soldiers. The remains came non-stop by transport planes, trucks, or Chinooks. Then they went to the mortuary to be identified to be sent back home to their families. A few months later, they had me help in the mortuary. The dead bodies kept arriving as in a never-ending nightmare."

"Some of the dead bodies were charred beyond recognition. Some remains were mutilated with limbs missing or large portions of their bodies gone. Some faces were scary looking since they were so mutilated. Some bodies were covered with maggots. A few were totally intact as if they were sleeping. The dead corpses had a rank and pungent smell like rotting garbage.

---

61   Cam Rahn Bay, http://pcf45. com/cam-rahn/camrahn. html

The smell of the dead never left you, no matter how much you washed your hands or clothes. The skin was cold to the touch. The eyes bulging out of their sockets, starring at you without moving. Their tongues were swollen and protruding. Rigor Mortis had set in, and the body is stiff and bloated to twice their size. Their skin discolored to a purple/black color. Since I've been home, I haven't been able to sleep. The bodies keep reappearing in my mind, over and over again. I knew I could never go back again."

When Denny's mother Helen, died in February 1968, he was given a temporary leave home. After being home for a week, he decided to go AWOL and not return to Vietnam, even though he only had 45 days left in country.

AWOL is abbreviation for away without official leave (absent without permission).

Being AWOL for 30 days is considered desertion. During a time of war, the death penalty may be applied. But if you voluntarily return, reduced punishment can be negotiated, and mitigating evidence can reduce the severity of the punishment. After 30 days, our friend Ray tried to convince Denny to turn himself in, but he refused. Denny had no plans to ever go back to Vietnam and thought he would never get caught. How he got caught was comical and befitted Denny's personality.

Denny and Ray's brother Joe were on their way to a job interview at a steel plant, when they were pulled over by a police officer. Joe is surprised by this and says to the officer, "Good morning officer, was I speeding?" The officer responds, "No. Can you tell me what shoe size you and your friend wear?" Joe is amazed to hear this question and says, "I wear a size 9 and my friend wears a size 11." The officer then says, "I want you to follow me back to the police station and don't try to get away." At this point, Denny is thinking they must know about him being AWOL and they plan to arrest him. He starts plotting a makeup story.

At the police station, the officer says, "There have been many break-ins in the neighborhood and you two match the description of the suspects." Before the officer can complete his story, Denny says to him, "Officer I'm here on leave from Vietnam because my mother just died, and Joe and I are not even from this area. We are going to a job interview at the steel plant down the road."

The officer questioned them further, cleared them, and let them go. However, Denny has peaked the officer's interest and he checks out his social security number and finds a note about him from the FBI. He contacts the FBI, and they arrest Denny at the steel plant. He was given a dishonorable discharge, forfeiture of all pay, and spent several months in confinement.

Because of what Denny saw, he struggled with Post traumatic stress and turned to drugs for relief. He started slowly smoking marijuana but later turned to heroin. He was never the same happy person I knew before Vietnam. Denny had just broken up with his girlfriend Rene that he had dated before we left for the Army. Rene couldn't deal with the "new Denny." In 1971, Denny moved far away from the neighborhood to escape from his many drug using friends, that included Geno.

In April 1969, Billy was home from the Army after serving a year in Vietnam. When he first went in, he was assigned to Germany, but wanted to see action and he requested, and received, a transfer to Vietnam. He served with the 23rd Infantry Division, the Americal Division, who operated in close cooperation with the 1st Marine Division in the northern part of South Vietnam.

During the 1968 Tet Offensive, they fought along the 1st Marine Division in fierce fighting again the Viet Cong and North Vietnamese elements. During the Tet-Offensive, the Viet Cong and North Vietnamese Army, overran the city of Hue. From January 31, 1968, to March 2, 1968, Billy's unit, with the 1st Marine Division, fought to regain control of the city. There was bitter street fighting and hand-to-hand combat. Hue was finally recaptured after many were killed.

One of those killed during the fighting, was a marine named Ben. Billy and Ben had gotten very close and become best friends since they had so much in common. Billy was talking to Ben at Hue when Ben was shot by a sniper in the face. The bullet took off part of his face.

Billy frantically tried to save him. He wrapped his shirt around his face as he tried to stop the bleeding, yelling for a medic. The medic arrived in a few minutes, but it was too late. Ben died in Billy's arms. This caused Billy to hate the Viet Cong and swore to kill as many of them as possible. He became very unhappy with life and a much more violent person.

When Billy came home from Vietnam, he was suffering from PTSD but didn't know it. He was having nightmares and if a helicopter ever came overhead, Billy would panic, run into his house and yell, "Incoming."

I didn't realize how violent Billy had become after Vietnam, until that afternoon in 1969, when he came pounding on my door. I find him panting frantically as he struggles to talk. There is blood on his shirt and he's holding a baseball bat that is split almost in half. I'm shocked to hear him say, "I think I just killed Tony."

Billy's mother had divorced his stepfather a few months ago and Tony was her new boyfriend. Tony, recently released from prison, was a huge specimen of a man and more aggressive than a female bulldog in heat. Billy hated him but was afraid of getting hurt if he got into a fair fight with him.

I said, "You got into a fight with Tony! Are you nuts." Billy laughs and continues, "I walked into the 41st bar and there was my mother sitting on a bar stool next to Tony. They had their backs to me and didn't see me walk in. I found out a few days ago that he had beaten my mother so badly, that she was covered in blood with a black eye. Before they could turn around, I left the bar and headed to my car to get my baseball bat. Then I went back to the bar and there he sat with his back to me. I got behind him and hit him squarely on the back of the head. It hit with such a force that the baseball bat nearly split in two.

He's bleeding badly but still breathing, so I went for the final blow. But my mother stepped in between us and yelled, "Stop Billy, you're gonna kill him." I ignored her, swinging at his head, but she put her hand up and blocked most of the swing. Blood is streaming out of his head. People are screaming and yelling, "Call the police" or "call 911." I got scared and ran out of the bar to your house." I had Billy call his stepfather and he convinced Billy to turn himself into the police.

Billy's mother probably saved her boyfriend's life when she blocked the potential final blow. However, she did suffer three broken fingers. Tony was seriously injured and airlifted to a nearby hospital. He suffered a fractured skull and bleeding on the brain. Tony took several weeks to recover. Because of Billy's savage attack on Tony, the police arrested him on suspicion of causing grievous bodily harm, but his mother convinced Tony to drop all charges.

In 1971, life was quiet in Billy's life, and he moved in with his mother and Tony. But it was only the calm before the storm. Even though Tony had forgiven Billy for the previous attack, Billy was convinced he was only laying low and would attack him when the time was right. Billy plotted and waited for the right moment to attack Tony again. The opportunity presented itself when Tony was taking his customary Saturday night bath:

As Tony lay soaking in the tub, Billy attacked him with a police baton he kept for protection. He hit him over and over, and soon the clear water of the tub was changed to bloody red. Tony was unconscious and Billy ran away thinking he had killed him. Billy's mother found Tony a few minutes later and he was taken to the hospital. He spent several months in the hospital and refused to press charges against Billy. However, he had enough. He was now terrified of Billy and left his mother, never to be seen again.

I was discharged from the Army on August 1968 and within a few weeks I was back to work at the Ford Motor Company. There was no joyous reunion with Annie G. because I chose not to write her while in Vietnam. I'm sure I was quickly forgotten.

My life is tedious and dull. I lack motivation to do more than just exist. I work eight to ten hours, come home feeling exhausted and drained of energy, eat, and struggle to stay awake, before I doze off for an hour.

Then the scary nighttime arrives. I toss and turn unable to sleep. When exhaustion finally overtakes me, I wake up most nights in a deep sweat, as constant nightmares invade my sleep. The endless cycle repeats in the morning with no relief in sight.

Reports of snow falling creates anxiety and fear for me. Driving is so scary now. My pulse is racing, I'm shaking and sweating so bad as I drive, I think I'm having a heart attack. I feel like my life is in constant danger. I had to call off work several times when the threat of moderate snow makes me want to throw up. Reading is no longer possible. I read a sentence and my mind goes blank. I drift into the world of la-la land and remember nothing. I become frustrated as my mind wanders. I try to re-read, but the results are the same and I give up.

I think drinking is helping me cope with my problems, but insane rants and fits of rage, overtake me. So, I turn to a higher help called drugs. I start slowly with marijuana that gives me the mellow feeling I need. I especially liked driving after smoking a joint when I'm shit-faced. The stop signs always seem like they are a mile away and never get any closer. Then it is on to other types of drugs, but relief is nowhere to be found. I can't get back to "normal". I slowly start dropping out of the "normal" society and into the "hippie" society by growing my hair longer and wearing tie dye clothes like the hippies.

The phone rings at my mother's house, she picks it up and yells, in her broken English, "Fre dee, Ray knee wants talk with you." My heart is beating a mile a minute as I answer the unexpected call.

No one has taught me the rules of woman and dating. Prior to Vietnam, I was terrified of these wondrous and mystical creatures. My interaction with Vietnamese and Japanese woman in 1967, helped me to form some understand of the rules and woman. I thought I was figuring them out, but now I have to update my thinking, because American woman are much more complex.

"Hi Rene, what's going on?"

"Hey Freddy, I guess you know Denny and I are no longer a couple. He's so different now."

"I know. So, what are you going to do for a boyfriend now, since your kind of homely looking."

We both laughed at that. Rene is without a doubt, on a scale of zero to ten, a perfect ten. Many guys might call her a knockout, stunning, gorgeous, or breathtaking, but never homely. Rene is kind of like my best, and only, female friend. Because of my friendship with Denny, she off-limits. Even so, this is the first time she has ever called me at home, and it makes me feel good.

Rene was her Homecoming Queen at her high school, winner of several beauty contests, and now under contract as a model for some magazine. She is into hot looking guys. I didn't think I was one till I showed her my yearbook. She's looking through it to find the best-looking guy and kept turning pages till she got to almost the last page. Then she stopped at a picture." Wow! Who is this guy. He is super handsome." I was surprised to see that she was looking at me. But I do have to admit that my picture came out way better than it should have. "That's me. You knew that." She gave me a wicked little smile without answering.

We talked for hours. I was very surprised to hear that she has her own demons that are haunting her. I never expected her to have problems, thought it was only me. But now I find something interesting that I had not gave much thought to since Vietnam. And that something is women, and maybe I don't have to fear them.

"Freddy, looking good can be a blessing and a cruse. I have countless male friends, but almost no female friends. Many women, who don't even know me, hate me and won't talk with me. They think I'm a threat. That I want to take their man away, but I just want to have a female friend to talk with. I've stopped trying to make friends with women."

"I hate all the unwanted attention from random creepy men. They walk up to me and ask me for my phone number. Others whistle at me or honk their car horns. It is very stressful, and it scares me."

"Then there are guys that I want to approach me, but won't, assuming I will reject them. I want to yell at them, I'm lonely, please ask me out on a date."

After Rene hung up, it got me thinking about the unwritten rules of grading someone for "suitability" as a possible match for dating or friendship, and a filtering process to eliminate someone as a match or friend. So, I started developing my rules for "success with women."

I needed to start with a physical appearance rating system that is based on the "ten scale." Much of this is subjective to include more than just looks: Can't weigh more than me or be taller than 5' 5". Must have nice skin and teeth and nice feet, and so on and so on.

10 - Based on Rene's new information, there is no such thing. Rene's is now an 8.

8 to 9 - I think this is the top mark any woman can possibly achieve.

7 - solid number that might be closer to what I can best hope for since now I have to consider what women might rate me.

5- I'd hit it but won't date it.

3 - I think this is the lowest score anyone should ever get because they should get something for just "showing up."

Based on looks alone, I might be able to hit a 9, so that might initially mean that no woman would be out of my reach. But digging deeper into the true "10" rating that many women require of "tall, dark, and handsome", I could only meet two of three requirements since I'm not tall. And if you add in my emotional problems, you will think that might knock me down to a low from "six to even a three", but if you add in personality, wit, charm, and not to mention the "bad boy thing", I could be a solid seven to many women.

So now I had to have some "subjects" to test my scale and refine by adding new factors after I have more feedback from other woman. Of course, I can't tell them about my rating system, so getting feedback might be hard to get.

For the next few months, Rene calls me at least once a week. We talk about various topics. One day, out of the blue, she asks,

"Why don't you ask me out?"

"I would if not for Denny being one of my best friends."

She never brought up the topic again. She told me about the several "LSD trips" she had taken and felt that her body wasn't good enough.

"Freddy, my body needs a tune up. I'm getting a boob job."

"That's gross Rene. You don't need fake boobs. That would be bad for your health. Silicone gel can leak into your lungs and liver."

And then she told me about her search for Mr. Right. She dated many guys, to include one of the Cleveland Browns starters, but had not yet found the right guy. She did say that one guys might be in the running.

I had not heard from Rene for nearly a month, so I was happy to hear from her again.

"Hey Freddy, are you home now?"

"Yeah, I'm here."

"Great. Don't move I'm coming right over. I have a surprise to show you."

She shows up at my house with a brand new 1969 Corvette. Written on both sides of the vehicle is, "Miss Chevy Hot Pants." When she gets out of the car, the only words out of my mouth were, "OMG."

Rene is wearing blue Hot Pants with black knee-high boots and a white see-through tank top.

"Hey Freddy, I just won this Corvette because I was chosen "Miss Chevy Hot Pants."

"What do you think?"

"You look great, even with your fake boobs, and that car isn't bad."

"Do you want to drive it."

She let me drive the car around for a spin and we get quite a few stares, and many heads are turning. Before she leaves, she says in typical Rene fashion,

"See what you're missing, this could of all been yours. Since you missed your opportunity, I'm gonna give you a shot with one of my best girlfriends."

In 1969, Rene introduces me to one of her best friends, Audrey, an airline stewardess. She is a solid "8", very beautiful with a great figure, and a great personality to match. And as an added bonus, Rene says she is a virgin.

In order to date her, I had to go through an old fashion process. I have to go to her house and sit upstairs with her family, to include her grandmother, and let them judge me. This ritual will go on till Audrey and her family accept or reject me. It took nearly two months, but I was finally accepted by Audrey and her family.

About the same time that the courting process was going on, my friends informed me that a young lady in our group, named Nancy, had developed a crush on me. I couldn't think of who Nancy was, till someone pointed her out to me.

She is attractive, but very quiet. I asked her out on a date and found out that she had moved here from Detroit and was a huge baseball fan. So that moved her rating up from a 6 to a possible 7.

But she is very outspoken and at times she turns me off, knocking her down to the 5 range. I felt it would not take much to push her down to the 3 area.

During this same time, I would see Audrey from time to time. However, things got very complicated when Audrey informed me that she was in love with me.

While I considered Audrey wife material, and that she was perfect for me, I was not ready for marriage. So, I decided to break up with Audrey and continue on my relationship with Nancy.

Her family thought I had disrespected Audrey and her brothers and cousins vowed to make me pay for this disrespect. It was lucky for me that Audrey had another suitor waiting who quickly pursued her. In a few months they were married, and I was quickly forgotten.

I was back with Nancy in 1969, but things were not going well. Nancy was quickly becoming a turn off for me. One day she unceremoniously dumped me in front of several friends. Shortly thereafter, I heard that Nancy was at some nightclub throwing herself at some singer in a band. I was glad to be rid of her and had lowered her rating to a low 3.

After Nancy, there was a long series of women in my life, all 5's or lower with one exception:

There were the crazy and aggressive woman: Christy who I thought was mentally unstable; Kathy the RN who tried to put me in headlocks and stalked me after I dumped her; Fran, who didn't act very nice after I broke up with her. There were the willing barmaids: Kathy, attractive and fun, might have worked if not for her past; the others were just "something to do" and I remember almost nothing about them. There were the sisters and the friend of a sister: The sister and her sister-in-law that barely rated above a 4. The other two sisters that were like night and day, neither of which I liked much.

Within this group, was a friend of a sister. She was a solid "7" that night, and I woke up with her in the morning after a hard night of drinking. I could of really liked her and I regret not pursuing her further. I just wish I could remember her name and what attracted me to her.

There were many other nameless women: The married woman, with three kids who was cheating on her husband. She "visited" me every Friday. Within a month she was telling me, "I'm in love with you."; The two close friends who were fighting over me; The single woman who turned out to be married; and so, on and so on.

I'm now very frustrated with woman and dating. I thought they might provide some relief from my problems, but instead they are adding to my frustration and hopelessness. I have to come up with something beyond just physical measures, so I created a new layer of rules called "accept or reject" that includes subjective factors such as personality, values, and traits.

Starting with reasons to reject someone: Aggressive or violent behavior, controlling, unreasonable, compulsive liars, talks too much, talks too little, too old, too young, not into her, always late, married, mentally unstable, smoker, too emotional, and she's not into me.

Reasons to accept someone: She's into me, she is intelligent with a nice personality, she likes sports, gambling, and travel. She is somewhat of a religious person, she works for a living, she is honest, interesting to talk with, faithful to me, we get along very well, and I'm sexually attracted to her.

Well now with these new rules, I was certain that my life was about to get better. All I need is more test subjects. By then everything changed again.

In January 1969, my father passed away from emphysema. It was a horrible thing to watch him suffer because he couldn't breathe. Many times, he would say to me "I can't breathe, I don't want to live anymore, I want to die."

He was down to skin and bone. He had to have oxygen to breathe but I didn't help him much. I felt like I was not there for him, but I was having my own issues with Vietnam.

At the funeral, people are distraught, grief-stricken, and crying endless tears. But I feel separated from the world. I feel like I'm watching from afar. I'm indifferent to their pain. I feel no pain, no sadness. No tears flow from my eyes. I sit stone-faced, rigid. I'm unfazed by death. I'm out of place here. I'm living a cruel curse that seems to have no ending for me.

Days after my father's funeral, my Uncle John's 3rd wife, Aunt Rosa calls and we have a very ugly exchange. My Uncle John is dying of cancer and will soon join his other siblings, my father, Uncle Corwin and Aunt Jessie, into the everlasting. This would then leave my aunt Rosa as the sole Kirkpatrick remaining on that side.

She is screaming at me, "Your mother took advantage of your father and made his life miserable."

"She goes to Guatemala to protect her secret that he is not the father of Rose. Then she lies to him about it. And there are more evil secrets that she is keeping."

Before she can tell me more, I yell back at her, "Your Nuts!" and hang up on her.

With me hanging up on her, I have lost all connection to the Kirkpatrick side of the family. But she brought up things that I suspected for a long time.

I did think it odd that my mother went to Guatemala for the birth of my sister. And where was my father. He was not there when she was born. It got my thinking about the night when he slapped my mother. Did he suspect something all along, or worse, did he find out about her secret lover.

I started to believe that Aunt Rosa's accusations against my mother were true and believed my mother was hiding other deep secrets. My loathe for my mother was now at an all-time high. My belief in women is now at an all-time low.

CHAPTER 9

The Return to Normal

(Early 1971 - September 1982)

Early 1971 did not get off to a good start. It started with me getting fired from Ford Motor Company for destroying their property. However, the powerful United Auto Workers (UAW) union, got me reinstated after thirty days. The penalty was deemed too harsh for the offense.

This was a bit of a wakeup call for me. I stopped taking drugs and nearly stopped drinking. And it got me thinking about my future since I hated working in the foundry but had no other options.

At the end of 1971, I considered going to college and applied to seven colleges. Six colleges rejected me, but I was finally accepted at Cleveland State University to start September 1972.

I chose Management and Labor Relations for my major, the easiest route to a bachelor's degree in business. After graduation, I was certain that Ford would offer me a high paying white-collar job.

But the start of college was not without problems for me. My seven-year layoff from high school to college, put me at a huge disadvantage with the younger 18–19-year old's. I wasn't prepared for any math course and found them impossible. The heavy load of homework, tests and papers, created major stress for me that was affecting my health.

The day before a final exam, I would develop physical problems. At night, I would have horrible headaches that felt like my head was about to explode. By the morning, I had back pain that was so severe, I could hardly walk.

During lectures, I would be writing notes without any problem, but then out of nowhere, I would hit a "brain freeze." I would hear a simple word like animal, but my brain would freeze, and I couldn't spell it.

This would prevent me from completing the sentence. I would go into a panic because I was getting behind in my note taking. To keep moving, I would spell the word phonetically. So, animal might become "ann a mole." By this time my notes were a jumbled mess. So, a sentence might read something like this:

"I find wrdos jmbuled but mu bairn can fgirue out waht I'm syanig."

Then there were the women. I'm a 25-year-old guy surrounded by incredibly beautiful 18–19-year-old women. They don't seem to notice, or care, about the age difference. I should feel like I'm in heaven, but I feel so old and out of touch with them. I live in a world they can never understand. While I did get a few offers, I didn't date any of the college ladies during my freshman and sophomore years.

While I attended college, I took leaves from Ford as needed to attend college. However, Ford didn't like how I used their leave of absence to come and go as I pleased and still maintain my seniority and vacation time. So, Ford changed the rules that if you were going to college, you could only work during the summer months. In January 1975, job #1 at Ford was no more, I quit my job.

During one of my junior year classes in 1975, Maria, a 20-year-old Puerto Rican lady, walks in. She's cute, but not beautiful, wearing her long black hair in a braid. She completed the package with thick black glasses and a perfectly proportioned body. She complimented the package by being a straight A student and being completely devoted to all my wishes and desires.

I dated Maria throughout my junior and senior years. Not sure dating was the exact word for our relationship. After I quit Ford, my finances were very tight since I was living off a part-time job paying minimum wage. So, I rarely ever took Maria anywhere, but that never scared Maria off.

Maria was a solid "8" or "9", but when she let me know, she was madly in love with me, I broke things off that day, but never told her. After I dropped her off at home, I never called her, or saw her again.

In the winter of 1975, Cleveland hosted a ten-year reunion for Vietnam Veterans, in downtown Cleveland. The event included a large number of dignitaries and was billed as a "welcome home party" for returning Vietnam Veterans. Against my better judgment, I decided to attend.

During the ceremony, attended by several thousand Vietnam Veterans, a group of protestor punks showed up. They had long hair, were very young, about 18 yrs. old, and keep taunting us with chants of "baby killers."

So much for being welcomed back.

They were being protected by a large presence of Cleveland Police Officers, many of them on horses. Finally, the police had enough and "turned away" for a few minutes. Quickly, many of the Vietnam Veterans rushed the protestors and beat the crap out of these punks who quickly ran away.

I graduated from Cleveland State University on March 1976 with a degree in Management and Labor Relations, near the bottom of my class with a 2. 33/4. 00 G. P. A. My shortcomings in math were evident as I had failed three mathematics courses.

My expected job offers from Ford started with rejection. They said they only hire people with experience in Labor Relations. I got several job interviews through my college for sales position, but again no luck. After three months of looking, I settled for Job #2, selling life insurance on June 1976. It was now doing something I hated more than foundry work and making much less money.

During this time, many new nightclubs in the Cleveland/Parma area were drawing many singles together. On June 1976, I met Joyce at a nightclub. She was tall and had the looks and figure of a Marilyn Monroe. We dated for nine months, the longest relationship I had ever had. On April Fool's Day in 1977, Joyce played a cruel joke on me and broke up with me.

She said, "You're the coolest guy I have ever known, but I can't stand your coldness. You never kiss me or hold me. I can't even get you to hold my hand. You have no tender feelings."

Tears filled her eyes as I sit in muted silence, unable to experience her emotions. I was quite shocked to hear Joyce say things to me that I knew were true. Even so, a rage within me erupted. I started yelling at her, "Get out of my car."

She runs out of my car. It looks like tears are running down her cheeks. I'm looking at her in horrid disbelief, thinking, *"What is she crying about. She just dumped me. I should be the one crying. - as if a monster like me could."*

At another nightclubs in September 1977, I met Cathy. She had a modeling contract and on the weekends was on-hand to do promo events. The place was packed since all guys in the place would pitch their best lines to her in hopes of landing a date, or more. All would strike out. She was not here to date, but to increase business for the nightclub.

Beautiful woman doesn't intimidate me. I never had a problem approaching them. I was extremely confident that I could "read them" and say exactly what was needed. It was almost like a game for me to see if I could get their interest, their phone number, and then, victory. No further action would be needed.

After several months of weekly meetings at the club, I had accomplished my goal. Not sure why, but Cathy took a liking to me over anyone of the many hundreds in the club. But this time the hunter, became the hunted. I had lost. I had fallen for her. That was not in my plans. This was not supposed to happen.

Cathy was the most incredible woman I had ever met. Of course, she is stunningly beautiful, with a perfect figure, a perfect smile with perfect teeth, and perfect hair along with perfect skin. She always wears the perfect outfits, but it was her personality that got me.

Cathy had exposed a flaw in my rating system. I could find nothing wrong with her. What I had ignored in my system was an intangible called "falling in love." She was a "10."

At the final event, Cathy was asked to pick any guy out of the room that she wanted to dance with. This was the last event of the season since she would be heading back to her home in California. There were nearly 1,000 males at this event.

I stayed in the background knowing that even I had no chance with her. Then the moment came and OMG. She's pointing at me. I can't believe this is happening. Things have gone too far. She has fallen for me.

All the guys are straining to see who she is pointing to. I pretended to look the other way and she is left on the stage with no one to dance with. She looked stunned, but quickly recovered and pointed in another direction. I left knowing I would never see or hear from her again.

Deep emotions and closeness scared me. Many women tried to get close to me. But if they told me that they loved me, I would quickly end our relationship. I was like a corpse, dead inside, but still alive on the outside.

Cathy exposed my deep-seated problems. I wanted to love her but was afraid to show tender feelings. I couldn't overcome my fear of death - If I loved her, she would die like others I got close to in Vietnam. She would have tried to fix me, but I knew it wasn't possible.

I only lasted nine months on Job #2. On March 1977, I quickly jumped to another small insurance company before I could be fired. This second insurance company turned out even worse than the first company. Job #3 only lasted for eight months. At the end of November 1977, I was fired for poor job performance.

In December 1977, I was without a job and struggling to make ends meet. I was experiencing aches and pains, even though I wasn't doing anything strenuous. I had this buzzing sound coming from my right ear that drove me crazy. At night, I was having trouble sleeping. I would get up every few hours during the night.

My dishes are piled up in the kitchen. They have been that way for months. I feel so exhausted that I dread talking with anyone. I rarely go out or answer my phone. If the phone rings, I ignore it. It hurts too much to talk or listen. Even the simple task of eating exhausts me.

Today I've been sitting in my chair and can't get out of the chair. I'm too tired to talk or move. I'm paralyzed with depression. I can't get up so I've been sitting in my chair for hours. I can't move because exhaustion has overtaken me. My body has just shut down. I'm suffering from grief, sorrow, and sadness that I will never again see my friends. I struggle to remember when I was ever happy. Life seems hopeless. Nothing gives me pleasure.

My days are gloomy and dark. There is no sunshine, even when there is sunshine. I'm never happy, even when happy things are happening around me. I can't enjoy the happiness. I try to read but can't concentrate on the words. I start reading but my mind wanders, and I forget what I just was reading. I read the sentences over and over, but it does no good. I give up trying to read.

In January 1978, my good friend Tony was able to help me get job #4. I accepted a new position in sales and was now in retail selling furniture.

Early in 1980, Tony said he met the funniest girl in his lifetime. I asked Tony how he met her. Tony told me he was taking to Master Card about his bill and the lady on the other end, Diane, kept joking around with him. He said they talked for hours. He asked her out and they met the next day. A few months later they were married.

In 1980 I was entering my third year selling furniture. Things were going well. I was promoted to Assistant Manager with a possible chance of becoming a Store Manager and getting a huge raise. About the same time, Tony and Diane seemed to have made it their life mission to see me married. Tony said he had the perfect girl for me. She was one of Diane's best friends, a former cheerleader in high school. So, a blind date was setup to meet Barbara.

On the day of the blind date meeting, I was upstairs looking out my bedroom to get a glimpse of my blind date without Barbara knowing I was watching her. I see someone get out of Diane's car and she is more than I can hope for. She is slender with long blond hair. She is stunningly beautiful and I'm starting to fall in love.

She is also only 21 years old, while I'm eleven years older at 32. But surely, she won't be able to resist my great charm. After introductions, we all head out to the lake for our first "date". Tony and Diane come along to ease the tension.

I learn that Barbara has just graduated from nursing school as an RN and will start her new job in three months. However, the bad news is that she is off to Europe for a planned trip with her best friend. And even further bad news, I get the feeling she's not that much into me.

It was a long summer as I waited for Barbara to return from Europe and go on our first real date to an amusement park. The first date didn't go well. Barbara told Diane that she didn't want to go out with me anymore. But Diane begged her to give me another chance and Barbara finally agreed.

The second date we went to a movie, and I fell asleep in the middle of the movie and broke off my front tooth. All that seemed to amuse Barbara. The dating process went on for two years. We were married on Sept 1986.

Life was good. I thought I was back.

CHAPTER **10**

Struggling to be Normal

(End of September 1982 - February 1990)

A week before getting married on September 26, 1982, the VP of Operations from my furniture company met with me. He had planned to move me to a higher volume store, but I got into an argument about how they were promoting others from outside the company. I was fired from job #4. On our honeymoon in Florida, I was signing up for unemployment benefits.

A few weeks later, I got job #5 at Radio Shack making $5. 05 an hour selling computers and Radio Shack accessories. On August 1984, I quit before I could be fired for poor performance.

Early in our marriage, Barbara learned to live with my quick reaction to sudden movements. About a month into our marriage, Barbara learned the hard way when she snuck up behind me as she was trying to hug me. I flung her to the ground thinking I was facing a potentially life or death situation. My training in the Army helped me to survive Vietnam. But was now keeping me from living a normal life.

While working at job #5, Barbara and I discussed my future. We decided I should go back to college and work on a bachelor's degree in Computer Science. I applied to Kent State University and was accepted into the program. I elected to take the easier business side rather than the much harder development side because of less math courses.

It took 18 months and on May 1985, I graduated with a bachelor's degree in business with a major in Computer Science, and a 3. 33/4. 00 G. P. A. , I was certain that I would get a job as a Computer Programmer. But as luck would have it, the personal computer wave had begun and very few computer programmers were needed.

While looking for my next job, I was working part-time at a cable company, selling upgrades to their lineup by adding Showtime. I was very good at the job and soon was the top salesman in the company. The cable company liked me so much that they were going to promote me.

I was very happy with my part-time job, but along came an offer from 3M in October 1985 to sell office equipment. I quickly accepted job #6 with a dream come true company. The first week in January 1986, I was on my way for two weeks in training to the twin cities of Minnesota.

Just before I was to leave, our beautiful daughter, Claire, was born on January 2, 1986, at 2:43 AM. I still remember when I first held her how she was licking her lips and looking into my eyes. It made me want to cry. I was deeply in love.

My two-week training was over and as soon as I arrive home, Barbara is leaving back for work after her six-week maternity leave. I'm handed my small bundle of joy, my beautiful six-week-old Claire. I was given instructions to call Barbara's mother if I run into trouble.

Almost as soon as Barbara leaves, Claire started crying. I tried everything I could think of to make her stop: Burp her, feed her, change her diaper. Nothing helped. She kept on crying, nearly two hours until I called Barbara's mother begging for help. Within a half-hour, Barbara's sister Donna arrived, took baby Claire and just like that she stopped crying. I was soaked in sweat as well as Claire.

During the first year at 3M, I was building a huge backlog of possible sales, but actual sales were slow in happening. This was not good enough for my 3M Manager and I was fired from job #6 on October 1986 for poor performance.

A few months prior to being fired from 3M, I had applied to Case Western University to begin a quest for an M. B. A. in Marketing. I was very surprised to be accepted to one of the top twenty-five business schools in the country. I started the program in August 1986, but now I was again without a job.

On September 1986, I saw an ad in a veteran's magazine that caught my eye. Mrs. Bolen Sr. asked if anyone knew her son, Jackie Bolen Jr. , killed on October 17, 1967, with the 2/28th "Black Lions" of the 1st Infantry Division. This seemingly innocent ad took me back nearly twenty years to a horrible battle that I had locked out of my mind for so many years.

I had blocked out almost everything about that battle, so I wasn't sure I knew her son. I decided to write her and ask if she could send me a picture of Jackie. The family sent me his picture and their contact information.

I really wanted to help this family, but I was struggling to bring back details about the battle and couldn't recognize him. It had never occurred to me to think about how others were feeling about the battle and felt very hopeless that I was unable to help.

I talked to the family via the sisters of Jackie and let them know I would stay in touch and try to find someone that knew Jackie.

Their mother, Betty, was still too heartbroken to talk about her son.

On December 20, 1988, I received a letter from Mike Dinkins that would draw me back further into the battle. Mike and I were both in Vietnam in 1967 with the same company. He was also transferred to the newly formed Delta company around July 1967. But unlike me, Mike was back at the NDP on the radio listening to the massacre that would leave him deeply traumatized by the experience.

The massacre of the 2nd Battalion of the 28th Infantry Division, was both shocking and unexpected. The battle, comparable to Custer's Last Stand,[62] led to 59 US deaths and 71 others that were wounded in action.

Officers in the General Staff of the 1st Infantry Division, refused to admit it was an ambush, called it a meeting engagement and told the media that the battle was a major American victory. [63] They also drastically inflated the enemy losses at 103, [64] even though the number was no more than 22. [65] Major magazines such as Newsweek, [66] and Time, [67] reported the number of VC at the battle around 300-400, not the full regiment number of 1200-1500. [68]

Mike was doing research on his Baccalaureate Thesis at the Evergreen State College in Olympia, Washington. He was attempting to reconstruct the events of the ambush of the 2/28th on October 17, 1967. I was immediately interested and contacted Mike. He sent me a ton of information about the battle, and I got deeply involved.

This led me on a quest to identify all fifty-nine of those killed, to contact the families of those who were killed, and to find the survivors to construct the original Delta and Alpha companies from 1967.

In 1989, I was in contact with Clark Welch, my company commander with Delta company. He told me that he remembered Jackie Bolen Jr. very well and would like to talk with the family.

---

62   Custer's Last Stand, www. americaslibrary. gov/jb/recon/jb_recon_custer_1. html

63   Email October 21, 2007, from an Officer with the 1st Infantry General Staff

64   Captain Cash interview of Captain Thomas Suttle on November 19, 1967

65   VC killed per After Action Reports conducted after the battle

66   "Ambush of the Black Lions", Newsweek, October 30, 1967, p 21

67   "A Sudden Meeting", Time, October 27, 1967, p 24

68   VO Minh Triet, David Maraniss, "They Marched Into Sunlight, p 159

I also found another Delta soldier who remembered Jackie. The family was very happy to hear from him and Clark Welch. That same year, I located, and visited, Gary Lincoln's family in Eaton, Ohio.

Gary Lincoln was one of six from my squad that was killed on October 17, 1967.

When I was looking at the index of those killed in Vietnam during the month of October in 1967, I was surprised to not find the name of Willie C. Johnson Jr. I thought maybe somehow, he had survived. I located a cousin in Atlanta, Georgia and she confirmed that he did pass away, but it wasn't until November 9, 1967. She did put me in contact with his stepson, but he did not seem that interested.

The most incredible story of survival from the battle was Willie C. Johnson. He held on until he finally passed away on November 9, 1967. It makes me sick that he was never awarded a medal for heroism. I thought he deserved at least a Silver Star.

On November 1986, I landed job #7 with a small electronics company close to home. My boss was a jerk, the pay lousy, so staying at Case Western would be too expensive. I made plans to continue my studies at the less expensive University of Akron.

By the end of 1988, my company promoted me to buyer. Now I had a career path in front of me. I started looking for a buyer's job so I could increase my salary. By September 1989, I was offered a buyer's position with a large increase in salary. My company was not happy when I quit job #7.

I started my new position as a buyer on October 1989. My new company was awesome. It was a very fun group with many Vietnam Veterans. I quickly became very good at purchasing as I studied and applied newly acquired buying techniques.

However, I was difficult to get along with. I would take unimportant events and turn them into potentially life-and-death situations, such as the following:

Someone in shipping missed a shipment and that caused us to be late in shipping an order to a customer. I headed down to the shipping department in a rage, my face flushed in anger. When I found the women who caused the problem, I started screaming at her, "Why Didn't You Get This Done On Time. You've Missed Our Shipment. You Have To Do This Right 100% Of The Time Or Someone Might Die Because Of You."

In February 1990, our second beautiful daughter, Eliza, the winter baby, was born.

CHAPTER 11

From Good to Horrible

(March 1990- June 2004)

During the summer of 1991, I saw an old friend from Vietnam, Roy Key from Tennessee. I told him about all the problems I've been having since my return from Vietnam. That I was having trouble sleeping, the nightmares, the anger, the rage, the drinking, and the drugs. I say to Roy, "I'm a troubled and crazy person."

Roy says, "Fraed, you're not the only one with problems after Vietnam. Two weeks after I got back from the Nam, I married my childhood sweetheart. I used to go to church regular like and met this gal who was the preacher's daughter."

"Fraed I knew right off that something was wrong with me. I wasn't the same person but didn't know why. Soon enough we had our first child. My wife knew something was wrong. She said to me, "Your distant, not happy go lucky as before."

"Fraed I just wanted to be left alone. I started smoking pot and juicing me with lots of drinkin to forget." Roy continues, "I had a short fuse over little things - like the baby crying in the crib while I'm trying to sleep. I said to the baby, "shut up and shook her a little. This scared me and my first incline that something was not right."

"Fraed I would have never known what the problem were if not for my back problems that I got from jumping out of one of them their helicopters in the nam. I went to the VA, and they said I had PTSD problems. But it was too late, my marriage was over."

"Hey Fraed, You all remember Griego from our Delta company?"

I said, "Yeah I remember him Roy, he was shot up on the 17th. Wasn't he in your platoon?"

"Yeah. He'd been having problems till he got help from the Veterans Administration. Over the years he had been in contact with twelve others we had been in Vietnam with. They were also in that battle on the 17th, and all had problems. Two of them boys killed their selves. Another one had massive heart attack at forty. Bout that time he had three bad marriages and been in jail for ten years."

After being at job #8 for over three years as a buyer, I was frustrated and wanted more responsibility and more money. Right about this time, my boss, the Purchasing Manager, quit and that position became available. I was the leading candidate.

However, the Material Manager was also promoted and that created the position I really wanted. But there was another candidate with a stronger background and she got the job. I now had a decision to make. Take the Purchasing Manager job, with a nice increase, or move on to another company. I decided to make a move to another company and quit job #8.

Barbara had been nagging me for years about my problems, (constantly) telling me I need to get help. So in 1993, I decided to get help with my problems because of my service in Vietnam. I went to a VA hospital to see a psychiatrist. He found I was suffering from severe Post-Traumatic Stress Disorder (PTSD). [69]

Post-Traumatic Stress Disorder is a mental condition that can develop after a person is exposed to traumatic events or threats on a person's life.

---

69   U. S. Department of Veterans Affairs, National Center for PTSD, www. ptsd. va. gov/public/ptsd-overview/basics/

During the years following Vietnam, veterans returning from combat with symptoms of insomnia, recurrent nightmares, depression, guilt, and severe anxiety, were termed "Vietnam combat reactions." The term was later changed to Post-Traumatic Stress Disorder. [70]

On August 1993, I accepted job #9, a Purchasing Manager job that was nearly an hour drive each way. It was a small foundry company run by Frenchmen that hated Americans, thought they were stupid and lazy. And the Americans hated the French and thought them arrogant. I now had the title "Purchasing Manager" that I needed to further my career.

The French were losing money and had to let nearly everyone go, including me, to make the bottom line look better so they could sell the company. So, on September 1994, after 13 months, I was fired from job #9.

On November 1994, I accepted job #10, a Material Manager position with a very small company. This was also a long drive from home and another awful boss; however, it was a great learning experience and added a much-needed title to my resume.

I was only using this company to land a better job with a shorter drive and more money. Within seven months, I landed job #11. This was a great position as a Purchasing Manager with a large company, only a 15-minute drive. I also got a very nice raise with an awesome boss who I liked and respected.

It had taken me six years, since my first job in purchasing, and four moves, but I was able to double my salary in that short time frame. I started my new job in May of 1995. Life was very good.

By 1996, my deep depression gave way to bundles of uncontrollable energy. I rambled as I talked in a rapid-fire manner, changing topics frequently. My mind was spinning in circles. My thoughts are racing, and I can't get the words out fast enough to complete a topic.

---

70   Historical names for PTSD, operationcompassionatecare. org/historical-names-for-ptsd/

I race from one subject to another, quickly losing my train of thought. I try to slow down my rapidly moving mind, but I'm unable. I can't concentrate on one task, so I ramble through multiple tasks, completing none of them.

With all this energy, I get deeply involved with the Internet part-time, while I held down my full-time job. I'm sleeping only a few hours a day, creating thousands of websites. Within a few months, I'm selling products all over the world.

Because I was on edge a lot, I would overreact to stupid things on impulse. I would be watching television and Claire and Eliza would be playing in the house. They were running and screaming as they play. The dog is running and barking as she joins in the fun. However, my head is exploding.

I finally have enough and get up yelling, "Stop that screaming." The girls ignore me and I go crazy. I take my belt off and run after them, hitting furniture near them. They run screaming in terror as they bolt for their rooms. I put my fist through a picture in our living room, shattering it. My heart is racing as I try to bring myself back to control.

During the winter months, I was scared to death when Barbara would leave for work in a snowstorm. I would be in a state of panic thinking that she will die in the storm. I would not be able to relax until Barbara would call me from work.

At night, I would lock all doors and windows. For added protection, I put a chair against the door handle. If someone breaks in this will give me enough time to shoot them. So, a loaded handgun is always within inches of me. Two other handguns are hidden in the home for back up. Of course, I don't tell Barbara about the handguns. I'm up many times during the night to make sure we are all safe.

From June 1997 to December 1997, I went through an experimental PTSD program, deemed to be the best in the country.

For me it was a long hateful struggle with a program that didn't work and brought about a profound hatred of the VA system. I thought I would be getting individual therapy but was instead forced into group therapy with veterans I had nothing in common with.

None of them had ever been in combat and crybabies that were "overacting" their "problems." Then came the monthly letters from the VA about losing statements of my problems I had sent them. My therapist pushed me to the edge one day when he said he didn't think I was "violent", according to their new program.

I went crazy and started screaming at him, "You want proof, how about I send you two boxes with two dead heads in them. You pick whether you want animals or humans." He looked stunned, didn't answer and left. A few days later I was given a new therapist because the other one said, "I'm scared of this guy." A month later, I dropped out of the program.

The eventual loss of my job #11 began in 2003. A new regime was appointed, and my boss was forced out. They then turned their attention on trying to force me out. They started with humiliation by yelling at me for leaving early and firing my secretary while I was sent out on a project.

Then my starting and ending hours were changed. Finally, they moved me from my large office area to an isolated tiny office in the basement that was a converted toilet. When I didn't quit, they moved me to corporate headquarters and took almost all my responsibilities away. I was not going to quit no matter what they did, they would have to fire me.

What brought things to a head was when I went to a Free Psych exam for employees having problems with work. The Doctor claimed it was a "confidential" exam. I told this doctor that I wanted to "kill" my two asshole bosses from the new regime. What I didn't know was that this doctor had to report to my company that I wanted to kill my bosses.

At the end of May 2004, less than a month after the "confidential exam", I was fired from the job I held for nearly ten years. Just before my firing in the afternoon, there a "blood bath" in another section of the company with the firing of an entire department. They had no warning and were all crushed by the news. Many left crying and wondering what they would do to repair their torn lives.

By early 2004, my 22-year marriage had hit an all-time low and I could not do anything to change it. I think we both knew our marriage was over. During this time, Barbara told me she hated me and things got ugly. Daily she would tell me she wanted me out of the house.

Soon all of Barbara's relatives and friends turned against me. Then the neighbors shunned me with their looks, tone of voice, and behaviors. I no longer felt safe or welcomed in my neighborhood. My daily morning and afternoon walks in the neighborhood had to be done when few neighbors were outside. And my daughters were not happy with me and ignored me most of the time. Only our cat would "talk" to me.

During this time, I'm having two recurring nightmares. In one dream, I'm buried alive in a coffin. I'm suffocating as dirt is falling in on me that is sucking the air from my lungs. I'm grasping for air as the dirt is choking the life out of me. I try to dig out of my coffin, but the dirt keeps falling on me. I wake up screaming, grasping for air like a drowning man.

In the second nightmare, I'm looking at a deep well and stumble backwards into the well. I'm falling faster and faster, plunging straight down towards a swinging pendulum blade. Seconds later, unable to stop my movement, I feel the horrible pain in my back, as the razor-sharp blade impaled through my torso. I bolt up, fully awake from my deep sleep. My body is drenched in sweat and I'm shaking uncontrollably.

While the divorce proceedings were going on, Barbara and the girls left for a few days. It was the first time I had been alone at night in our two-story colonial. The empty house felt like it was five times bigger than before they left. At night, noises were everywhere. I couldn't sleep. I had my . 38 revolver on the bed with a box full of ammo. I kept the weapon unloaded when the girls were home.

Just having the weapon next to me made me feel safe. Sometime after midnight, I fall asleep. Around 2 a. m. , I'm awoken from my sleep to movement outside our house. It sounds like someone is trying to break into the house. I get up immediately and reach for my revolver. I hear someone throw a chair through our front window and glass breaking everywhere.

I struggle to open the cylinder release latch because my hands are shaking so badly, and my heart is beating wildly. I'm struggling to load rounds into the cylinder. I get two rounds in the chamber, but I'm shaking so bad that I drop a few rounds.

Finally, I'm fully loaded and head downstairs to face the intruder. I move cautiously to the bottom of the steps and aim my revolver. I'm looking for the broken glass but find nothing. There is no sign of anything being disturbed.

My PTSD problems are worse than ever. Going back to October 17 and the events is driving me where I don't think I have anything to live for.

On June 3, 2004, I'm age 57, collecting unemployment benefits and my job outlook is not very good. I'm in a very bad place. I think I'm going insane, and that the VA is ignoring my problems. I'm plotting to "seize" the federal building in downtown Cleveland to get the VA's attention.

I'm planning to wipe out the 9th floor where all the reject letters are coming from.

CHAPTER 12

Ward 13

(January 2005 - September 2005)

January 2005 began my fight with squirrels for control of my backyard. They were boldly climbing up on our bird feeders, terrorizing birds, and feeding themselves at will. I devised many ways to try and prevent them from their free meals, but they always outsmarted me. As they are at the top of the feeder eating, they would mock me with their shitty-tooth grins as I looked hopelessly out the window. This outraged me and I quickly declared war on them, vowing to make their lives a living hell.

By February I found a Metal Squirrel-Resistant Tube Bird Feeder. I laughed as the squirrels rolled off the feeder, unable to reach the feed. This solved one problem but created another. The squirrels started feeding off the scraps on the ground, scaring off the birds. So, I would sneak up on them as they feed, killing several of them with a garden shovel.

The next day, one squirrel made the mistake of running onto our screened back porch when I opened the door. I quickly close the door, trapping the squirrel with no way out. I ran to the garage to get my garden shovel. I feel like I'm back in Vietnam during a firefight. I have the blank glaze of someone hypnotized in fear. My heart is racing, and fear is running through me. This will be a fight in which one of us will die.

With my shovel in hand, I enter the back porch door and quickly close it behind me. The squirrel screams in terror and tries to run away. I quickly corner it and it jumps at me with its sharp teeth. I swat it down with my shovel. The squirrel is dazed, and I run and stab it. I keep stabbing it till blood runs out and the squirrel lays dead.

Over the next few weeks, I continue killing. I kill several pigeons and even a few rats. I drown three skunks who have dug a hole in my backyard. And I run over squirrels as they play the dangerous game of chicken with me on the street. I'm thinking that maybe I'm in the process of a meltdown because I'm enjoying the killing. So, in late February, I setup an appointment to see my psychiatrist at the VA.

On my way to the appointment, I decide to take the turnpike instead of the normal route. As I'm nearing my destination, I come across this bridge that is suspended high above the ground, almost at tree top level. As I'm crossing, I imagine myself back in Vietnam in a helicopter just above the treetops.

I start to panic and feel that I'm going to go over the bridge and fall hundreds of feet into the concrete below me. I want to stop in the middle of the bridge and get out and save myself. I'm struggling to breathe and keep moving forward. I slowly try and get out of the curb lane and into the safety of the middle lane. Before I can do that, some car honks at me because I almost hit him. This brings me back to normal and I'm over the bridge.

I have been seeing Dr. Know Morgue for several months, but he rarely talks to me, and I didn't like him and never open up to him. Today he assigns my treatment to nurse Allie Holly. I feel comfortable with her and tell her about the problems I've been having. I tell her about the intruder I thought was in my house and the events that didn't actually happen.

What she said next startled me. She said, "You were having a flashback to something that happened in Vietnam and the memory was so powerful that you actually relived the experience in real time."

I thought, "How weird is that. I wonder what that event might have been."

I told nurse Allie about wanting to kill my bosses at work and how I think that got me fired. Then I told her about this man who was parked outside my house at night for about 30 minutes. This made me very uneasy, and I loaded my . 38 and pointed it at the car and the mystery man drove away before I could confront him. Everything seemed to be going well until I told her I have been killing animals over the last few months.

Her expression changes and she said, "Have You Told Dr. Know Morgue about killing animals?"

I said "NO", should I?"

She asked, "When are you seeing the Doctor next?"

I said March 21 and she said, "Make sure you tell him that you have been killing animals for several months." I said OK and left.

March 21 rolls around and I meet with Dr. Know Morgue around 11a. m. I'm hoping to be home by noon. Dr. Know Morgue asks me how I'm doing, and I said, "Fine, but the nurse wanted me to tell you that I've been killing animals."

His face changes, he looks pale and stunned. Then he goes off on me. "Why didn't you tell me this before." And then he picks up his phone and calls someone. I hear him say, "I need to admit someone today, do you have a bed?"

He hangs up and I say to him, "What's the Big Deal." Then he starts YELLING, "Killing animals is a precursor to killing people."

I'm thinking he has some mental issues. I've only been thinking of killing three people, my two ex-bosses and the idiot who parked in front of my house. And I haven't killed anyone yet.

I wonder what he thinks about hunters killing animals. Does he think they will be killing people?

Anyway, I say to him, "I have something to do, I have to leave now." He's got this dumb look on his face again and says, "You're not going anywhere. You will have to go to the psychiatric ward, maybe up to 22 days."

I can't believe this guy is saying this stuff to me. Soon two guys with a stretcher show up and ask, "Where is the patient?" Dr. Know Morgue points to me and they put me on the stretcher, strap me in and take me away. An hour later, at the VA Medical Urgent Care, I'm admitted to the Emergency room.

After a small wait, some attractive nurse comes up to me and says, "I will be processing you in. We will start with a physical exam to look at the problems you have been having." She adds, "Did anyone ever tell you look like Sylvester Stallone."I said, "I hear that often" and laugh.

I'm given a battery of tests to include a hearing test, X-Rays for my back, and a CT Scan of my head. All tests come back negative. The doctors determine the swirling sound is probably tinnitus. A blood test confirms that I have type 2 diabetes, probably from my exposure to Agent Orange.

Doctors also conclude that I'm suffering from a brain disorder associated with unusual shifts in mood, energy, activity levels, and ability to carry on daily tasks. Unlike my physical problems that are easier to treat, my diagnosis of being bipolar and deep depression, will be much harder to treat. I wonder how long I have been suffering from this deep madness, a silent killer of my thought process. To help me, they put me on medications, Paxil and Depakote, to treat my bipolar and depression.

After my physical, they have me wait in a separate room for hours. They say they are waiting for a bed for me. I'm sitting in the lobby for about an hour and some tall doctor says, "We will start checking you in very soon. You will be here about three days. It's voluntary and after three days you can leave."

Sometime around 11 p. m. , the tall doctor appears again and introduces himself as Dr. Jetlag and my bed is ready on the 3rd floor called Ward 13. He goes on to tell me that Ward 13 is an acute inpatient unit specializing in the treatment of mental illness and hands me a Patient Information Handbook. Again, he emphasis that this is a voluntary commitment on my part, and I will be here no longer than three days.

Since I'm so exhausted from what's been going on in my life, I figure that three days won't hurt, and the rest might do me some good. I sign the voluntary agreement to check myself.

What I didn't know was that I had just signed away my freedom.

I'm a little worried that Barbara might have me committed for life since she hates me and knows all these psych doctors.

Dr. Jetlag takes me to the 3rd floor, and we come upon two glass doors that are locked. He knocks on the door and some nurse comes running to the doors, let's us in and quickly locks the door again. The locked unit is about the length and width of a football field.

On my right side is the shower area and other closed doors. Also on this side is a phone attached to a big cord to be used by patients for calls in and out. As you walk on the right-side area there are two open room, both about 6' X 8'. One appears to be an exam room. The other room, called the seclusion room, is void of anything except for a mattress. There are no windows, and you can't see in or out. This room is used for difficult patients who get out of line.

Very prominently displayed in the center of the ward, is the Nurse's Station. It's a closed cubical area, 20 feet by 20 feet with door gates on either side. Inside is a small cage area with 3-5 nurses. The Patient Handbook states,

"The Nurses Station is for staff use only. Do Not Enter unless you are asked to do so."

Right next to the Nurse's Station is the Dayroom. It's about twice as big as the Nurse's Station and is the main hangout for the patients. There are about twenty chairs, various games and puzzles. Meals are brought in daily from downstairs and eaten in the dayroom.

Daily meals are one of the highlights during the day. However, the really big draw is the television. It's a small TV, maybe a 10" screen. You can only watch TV from 6:30 a. m. to 3 p. m. and again from 4 p. m. to 11 p. m. Program selection is by majority choice, either basketball or crime shows, neither of which I care for. The control of the TV is operated by staff or patients with staff permission. Only they can change the stations.

Next to the dayroom are six closed door rooms that are used by the important Ward Staff. They run down to the end of the hallway in the middle of the ward. At the very end of the hallway in the middle of Ward 13, is the dining room. It's a room slightly larger than the dayroom. It has a second TV and is much bigger than the one in the dayroom. Also in the room is a massive piano, a good size table with puzzles, many books, and a sofa and two chairs.

On the far-left wall of Ward 13 are sleeping rooms for the patients. The rooms are about 10' X 12'. Most of the rooms hold up to 4 patients, some two, and the lone room that holds one patient will be mine. I'm next to the Dining Room. Each room has a door, but the door can never be fully closed. It must always remain partially open for the half-hour night checks.

When you process in, you have no privileges, and you are restricted to the ward. You are not allowed to wear street clothes, shoes, belts, or have any sharp objects. Your daily uniform is top and bottom PJs with yellow slip proof socks. You can't have any personal items such as wallets, cell phones, car keys, jewelry, or money. These items are deposited into small lockers in the Nurse's Station.

You are required to always wear a patient I. D. bracelet. Quiet time on the unit is observed between 3 p. m. and 4 p. m. and again from 11 p. m. to 11:30 p. m. During that time, patients are restricted to their rooms to nap, read, or anything quiet. The televisions are turned off and telephones may not be used.

By the time I got checked in, it was nearly midnight. I head to my room for some sleep. As usual, I can't sleep and I'm up at 1:00 a. m. I head for the dayroom for about an hour until I get tired again. Things are very quiet on the ward. The nursing station seems to be the only place where life exists at this hour. I see one of the nurses' writing notes about me. She was probably noting that I was up in the middle of the night.

I wasn't expecting to find anyone in the dayroom, so I was surprised to see three patients up and engaged in a lively conversation. They are in discussions about "what is the most annoying sound you have ever heard." Chalk on the blackboard seemed to be winning, but the emergency alert system that interrupts your television shows and a baby crying are getting some discussion. I sit next to them. None of them act as if I am there. After about an hour, I'm feeling tired and head back to my room and sleep.

Sometime before 4:00 a. m. , I'm up again and head back to the dayroom. Again, that same nurse writes some notes about me. When I get to the dayroom, I'm very surprised to see the same three patients are up. I thought I was the only person in the world that had trouble sleeping at night. They are still involved in a heated debate and don't notice or acknowledge me. After about forty-five minutes, I'm feeling very sleepy and head back to my room to sleep.

Just before 7:00 a. m. , the lights in halls of the ward are turned on. A nurse is going around to the patient rooms to make sure everyone is up for meds. I'm up to take my meds and wait for breakfast at 7:30 a. m.

As I go over to the dayroom, I see a huge line at the nurse's station. It's the smoker's line as they wait for a cigarette to smoke during porch time at 7:15 a. m. The big highlight of the day for most is the three meals at 7:30 a. m. (breakfast), 12:00 Noon (Lunch) and 5:30 p. m. (Dinner). However, if you a smoker, the highlight of your day is porch Time at 7:15 a. m. , 9:15 a. m. , 1:15 p. m. , 6:00 p. m. , and 9:15 p. m. The name porch time is kind of misleading. "The Porch" is enclosed on all sides by steel bars. It is about 12' X 12'.

They are allowed only five cigarettes per day but are restricted to smoking on the porch. Some smokers told me they were so desperate for their cigarette, they would often skip a meal so as not to miss their smoke break. Others would beg non-smokers, to get a cigarette and pass it along on the porch. That was very risky for them since at least two staff members would guard and monitor the smokers every move. Passing of cigarettes was strictly prohibited. Anyone caught violating this policy could have their hair set on fire. But the penalty was even worse for the smokers, they would be barred for smoking for a period of one day.

Breakfast arrives at 7:35 a. m. and you have to wait in line until your name is called and then you can go up to get your tray. I'm disappointed to learn we are not allowed to have any coffee, sweets, or soft drinks. We have milk with every meal. I hope I don't go "crazy" from lack of caffeine.

Your entire day is structured. The Ward 13 daily schedule is as follows:

- 7:00 a. m. - Meds

- 7:15 a. m. - Porch time

- 7:30 a. m. - Breakfast

- 8:00-9:00 a. m. - Hygiene/Shave

- 9:00 a. m. - Meds

- 9:15 a. m. - Porch time

- 9:30 a. m. -11:30 a. m. - Meetings

- 12:00-1:00 p. m. - Lunch

- 1:00 p. m. - Meds

- 1:15 p. m. - Porch time

- 1:30 p. m. -3:00 p. m. - Meetings

- 3:00-4:00 p. m. - Quiet time

- 5:00 p. m. - Meds

- 5:30 p. m. -6:00 p. m. - Dinner

- 6:00 p. m. - Porch time

- 6:00 p. m. -9:00 p. m. - Meetings

- 9:00 p. m. - Meds

- 9:15 p. m. - Porch time

- 11:00 p. m. -11:30 p. m. - Quiet time

The cycle repeats daily and the patients like having someone control them, but I hate it.

As I'm eating my breakfast, I'm seeing some very odd people on the ward. Since I'm only here for three days, I need something to write what I'm seeing. Paper was easy to come get but I needed a pen to write with. When the nurses were not looking, I "borrowed" a pen. Then I started writing what I saw.

The strangest person I came across is this tall thin black man, about 40 years old. He walks around the ward but never says a word. I'm wondering if he can even talk. He has no clothes on, except for a diaper. I call him "the diaper man."

There is a young black male that has a strong resemblance to Muhammad Ali, so I nickname him "Ali." He's carrying a huge book, one of those 700-page reference type manual. I never saw him look at the book, so maybe it was just for show. I try talking to him. I ask him, "What are you reading?" He says, "I'm gay with a 12-inch cock." He leaves and walks out of the dayroom. He is muttering something, but I can't understand him.

The "chicken man" tells me he loves chickens and walks off.

A new patient has just entered the ward this morning. He's a white male, about 5' 6", wearing a suit and sunglasses, like an older Raymond from the movie Rain Man, but looks more like Charlie Babbitt. He didn't talk to anyone, so I never get his story.

After breakfast, I get my pills for depression at 9:15 a. m. The day drags on as I wait for lunch at noon. After lunch, I watch television, but after several hours of police crime shows, I take my leave for the dining room and hopefully some peace and quiet. I call the dining room my "secret room" since very few of the patients come down to this room. The hours are the same as the dayroom. The room is empty, and I work on a puzzle as I watch a show I like.

I'm alone for nearly two hours until "the diaper man" appears. He decides to stand right in front of the television. That doesn't bother me till he puts his hands in his diaper. This gets my blood boiling. I say to him, "Get the fuck out of here and go wash your hands." He quickly leaves and I don't see him again. After dinner, I retreat back to the dining room and work on my puzzle till its bedtime. This time no one bothers me.

Again, I'm up in the middle of the night, heading for the dayroom to see the three patients in the dayroom. This time there in a debate about, "What is the best space movie ever." The three are debating "2001: A Space Odyssey" against "Aliens" and it is getting heated with name calling. Again, the nurse is writing notes about me.

After an hour, I'm back to sleep for a few hours and head to the dayroom at 4:00 a. m. The same three are still in debate about space movies. Again, the nurse is taking notes on me. This time, after only 30 minutes, I'm feeling very tired and head back for some sleep. Just before 6:00 a. m. , I'm up and on to the dayroom. This time, I'm surprised to find that none of the three patients are up.

Day two starts out like day one. After lunch, I'm observing two other patients. The first is a short fat white male with thick black glasses. He reminds me of Charlie Brown from the comic strip Peanuts, so I nickname him "Peanuts." He likes to wear yellow PJ's size 2x or 4x. They are way too long for his short little body. He talks like a normal person, and I wonder why he's even here. But then he says something very odd, "I think you look like Barbara Mandrell."

She was an American female country singer on television during the 1970s and 1980s.

One of my favorite patients Jimmy, is a tall, thin, black male around 35 years old. Jimmy is always wearing the same jacket of his favorite team, the Dallas Cowboys. He loves to talk and soon I know his whole life story. Jimmy tells me he wants to move to Texas and that he loves prostitutes. His mother, the love of his life, owns her own store. He talks about his brother who is in jail, and that when he gets out, will join Jimmy in Texas.

Jimmy invites me to join them in Texas. Then he goes on to tell me how he's been in training for years to inspect houses and finally got his license to sell real estate. And for the last four years he's trained to do home design. Jimmy then shows me what he's learned these past four years. He's starts drawing his ideal two-story home that he plans to build in Texas. I'm expecting to see a very elaborate design. But I have to keep from laughing at the design he draws. It's a very simple two-story design that you might expect from a five-year-old.

After lunch, one of the nurse's comes up to me and says, "You have an appointment tomorrow at 8:00 a. m. at mystery door number four in the center corridor." Since that will be my third day on the ward, I'm expecting to be released. I'm super excited to leave.

The next morning, after breakfast, I head over to mystery door number four. I knock on the door and some nurse answers the door. As the door opens, I see about seven doctors and nurses seated in chairs around in a circle. My seat is to be in the center with a very large bright light shining in my eyes. Each of them goes around introducing themselves. I'm told this will be recorded as a training exercise for future psych students.

The first question they ask me, "Do You Know Why You Are Here?"

I answer, "I guess because I have killed a few animals."

The causes one of the doctors to say, "Killing animals is a precursor to killing people. You are here to make sure you don't do that."

Aside from killing dozens of innocent people, Jeffrey Dahmer, Ted Bundy, and David Berkowitz, and a significant percentage of serial killers, have something else in common; years before turning their rage on human beings, they practiced on animals.

According to the FBI, animal abuse is highly correlated with interpersonal, human-to-human violence. [71]

Then he asks me, "Are you thinking of harming yourself or others?"

I have to think about the possible consequences to me if I give the wrong answer. Since I'm not strapped to a lie detector, that might help how I answer. I certainly don't want to stay here longer than three days. Plus, I'm going through a nasty divorce with my wife, a Psych Nurse with many connections, so I'm scared she might have me committed permanently if I give the wrong answer.

I answer "NO". I don't think they believe me, but they accept my answer. Larry Broken, a social worker, gives his opinion about me.

He goes on to say, "I'm a Vietnam Veteran and know the pain your feeling because of your survivor guilt. You are a Walking Time bomb waiting to explode. You want to kill to feel better and then be killed because of the pain."

Larry Broken continues, "I want to work with you to get you into a six-month specialized hospital stay for PTSD patients. The first treatment part will be for six weeks, followed by another three-month program."

I now know these crazy doctors have decided what I have to do, and I better say "Yes" or stay on this floor for a very long time. When

---

71   Real Crime, January 03, 2018, Sarah Watts, https://www. aetv. com/real-crime/first-they-tortured-animals-then-they-turned-to-humans

I say to them that I will accept the help with my PTSD, everyone seems pleased. Some doctor tells me, "You will be released from the ward soon. I'm giving your "privileges" so you can leave the ward for an hour each day." That was exciting news since I will be able to buy things from the vending machines downstairs.

Later that day, we have a new patient admitted to the floor. And what a strange person he is. If you had only talked to him on the phone, you would think he was this huge Italian male about 6' 3" and weighs at least 220 pounds.

But in person, he is a short Italian male, 5' 2", that weighs 120 pounds. He has this very deep voice and I call him Foghorn. He is a nearly three pack a day smoker, so porch time is the best thing in his life. He smells terrible, his hair is mashed down with very coarse stubble on his face. He's also a very angry and paranoid person.

He tells me, "My wife had me committed after she claimed I assaulted her. He goes on, "She cheated on me, but my wife told a different tale. She said, "That's a lie. I've never cheated on you. You think all men are after me, but I only want you." Foghorn says, "My wife is bringing me clothes later." I can't wait to meet the woman that makes him so jealous.

After dinner, I've decided that tonight I'm going to find out more about my three late night patients. It's 1:00 a. m. , March 24, my fourth day on the ward. I'm heading towards the dayroom. My three mystery patients are all there.

I introduce myself, "Hi, I'm Fred a Vietnam Veteran." They start out by asking me why I'm here. I say to them, "I told my psychiatrist I was killing animals and they said I might kill people." That got a big laugh from them, and they nicknamed me "The Assassin."

The first patient to introduce himself is Dave. It's hard to keep up with Dave's conversation. He talks like he's on speed. I nickname him "Fast-talking Dave."

He reminds me of actor Philip Seymour Hoffman.

Dave is a white male, about forty-five, wears thick black glasses and is overweight for his short body. Dave says he's a two pack a day smoker and he's found a way to sneak in cigarettes to help his addiction. Dave goes on to tell me he has cancer, but the doctors don't believe him and they are trying to kill him by not treating him. Dave says, "The cancer is spreading all over my body and I'll be dead soon."

I ask Dave how he came to the ward. Dave says, "I was trying to stop the spread of cancer by drinking. Some voice tells me that the cancer is spreading to my brain. The voice tells me to kill myself before that happens because it will be a very painful death. My wife finds me passed out with a knife in my hand and calls 911 and they take me away."

While Dave is talking, I'm noticing one of the other patients mumbling to himself. I nicknamed him "The Mumble." His name is Jim. He is a tall, handsome, white male, about fifty with salt pepper hair. He says, "I was a sniper with the Marines in Vietnam. I had fifty confirmed kills."

I say to Jim, "Back in 1971 I was dating this gal for several months from a rural area about thirty minutes south of Cleveland. A few months into our relationship, she tells me that three guys in her town, are threatening her if she doesn't have sex with them. This sets me off and I hatch a plan to buy a high-powered rifle with a scope and kill them one at a time. I will do it from a roof top, near their apartment, in the middle of the night. The week before I was to set to kill them, I told my friend Tony. He thought I was kidding, but I told him they were going to die. Two days before I'm ready to launch my killing spree, my girlfriend says the three have left her alone."

Jim starts talking and says, "I know something about killing someone." Jim says, "I grew up in Chardon, Ohio with my younger sister and I have committed the perfect crime. At this point, I'm thinking Jim is making up a story to try and impress all of us, or just maybe he really did kill someone.

I ask him, "Can you tell us how you committed this perfect crime." Jim starts his long, rambling, detailed story of a perfect crime of murder:

"The deliberate description for unlawful gain is something we are all used to. But what about Fraud and revenge. Is our collective ability to ask proper questions an inability that provides a springboard for fraud, but not the execution of. Case in point. A nice guy visiting with Pennsylvania plates and no priors.

Veteran detective, Jim Nasium, pronounced gym-nasium, in a farming community in Ohio, is quizzing, why this guy with Pennsylvania plates on his car, was lying dead in the farmer's driveway. His sunglasses still clenched in his fist. Detective Jim Nasium watched as the dead man's car was hauled away from the dead man's bullet ridden body.

The farmer, who owns the driveway, farmhouse, a few cats for big dogs to chase, a 12-year-old very pretty daughter, as well as her mother. The farmer kept saying self-defense to Detective Jim Nasium. So, there is a problem with the dead man's civil rights and the farmer's right to defend himself.

The farmer's arrest with death penalty specifications seems too easy for the veteran Detective Jim Nasium, with twenty years' experience on the police force in Chardon, Ohio. The farmer only said self-defense, no matter what is asked or said to him. The farmer doesn't know what today's date is, so how can he assist in his own defense.

We now leave this rural location in Chardon, Ohio. The crime was done at 1 O'clock in the PM on September 1, 1999. The general reasoning process needs to be redone to solve this murder here. So let us travel to the start and a way away from the crime scene, and the writer's freedom of speech rights.

The farmer was a real lady's man in high school. Rumors abounded about his affair with an elementary aged girl then. Afterwards, the girl runs away to the streets of Los Angles. Farmer now has a younger daughter about the same age. The runaway has a younger brother, named Lou Gotu, who lives in the farmer's town of Chardon, Ohio and is a permanent fixture.

Lou Gotu has been at a gas station so long that he now owns it. The runaway sister is in rehab forever because of the love affair with the farmer and is elected by Lou Gotu in informal and formal charges.

The farmer every so often, would receive a death threat by phone and at the police station at the same time. The farmer owned a rifle for self-defense, if not for this lone reason for sure. The farmer's dogs make noise at night, and this helps him in his protective mode. But little does he know that the dogs are unable to help him or alert him for what awaits him. His Army training won't be able to help him as are the police unable to help. The nearest neighbors are miles away. There is a winding road in front, a lake stocked with fish is on the farm.

Lou Gotu won't be a tourist by choice, but rather avenging his sister who will forever be in rehab. "Killing Perfect by Fraud" is going forward for Lou Gotu. He caused the crime scene in the beginning, being investigated by detective Jim Nasium. The only witness to the crime is that damned scarecrow in the cornfield across from the farmer's house.

The plan went forward because Lou Gotu made the farmer pay for his sister in rehab by means of Pennsylvania. Lou Gotu numbered the scarecrow's days, and this consoled him because it also haunted him and not to doom him, he said to himself. Lou Gotu has criminal tools in the cornfield the day before the crime scene day beforehand. A sign reads "Free Puppies, Free Strawberries", but these two signs next to each other, near the road, across the street from the farmer's house, had metal sleds affixed underneath them and rope underneath covered with dirt. This would allow Lou Gotu, at the right time, to pull into cornfield.

The Pennsylvania motorist on the highway, turned into the farmer's driveway and was executed. Lou Gotu's method of operation was the criminal tools in the cornfield. The daughter was away with her mother.

Lou Gotu paid a local drunk to make a college fraternity prank call and threat to include the specific, I'll be there shortly to make good this threat and to reveal my identity at this time upon you alone. The local drunk was from Cleveland, Ohio and given bus ticket back with plenty of cash with his new address just in case Lou Gotu had to do to him what he has to do to that damned scarecrow to make perfect this planned crime

The drunk fulfilled the pledge of non-talking about fraternity pranks for legal reasons. The criminal tools were buried in a ditch in the cornfield beforehand by Lou Gotu. He said to himself, the jury must find the farmer guilty.

Lou Gotu went to work at the gas station and was ready to help the Chardon police during the day to discuss the farmer's temporary insanity pleas. The farmer pleaded temporary insanity but was not accepted by the jury and Lou Gotu said he believed in the temporary insanity plea for the farmer. He said to himself about scarecrow and getting to Cleveland, Ohio sometime before going back to visit his sister in the clinic."

It was quite a story and wondered if it was true. I called Jim's story the "Ramblings of a Mad Man."

I ask Jim, "Do you have a sister?" Jim would not answer, so I ask Jim, "Tell me how you came to Ward 13." Jim clams up and won't talk anymore and goes back to mumbling to himself.

The third patient is named Rodney. He is a tall white male, in good shape, very quiet, handsome, and around my age. Rodney said he served two tours in Vietnam with the Marines. So I call him "Rodney the Quiet Marine."

Rodney asks me, "Are you married." I said yes but I'm going through a messy divorce. Rodney says, "I'm divorced and have two daughters. My oldest daughter is a lawyer, very attractive, and you can't go out with her."

I thought that was an odd thing to say but did not reply to his statement. I asked Rodney, "How did you get on this floor." Again, he tells me the story of his two daughters and that I can't go out with his oldest daughter.

I finally decide to answer. "I'm not looking to date anyone." This seems to satisfy him. He goes on to say he was in his car and hit a wall. Then he changes the subject again. "I'm the copyright owner and protector of the story that follows public relations specific offerings. Also, I'm the patents pending owner and protector of items."

Then he goes back and repeats, "I was in my car and hit a wall." I ask him, "Why did you hit the wall". Rodney says his head hit the window and that he is diabetic and was in a diabetic state with low sugar. He tells the same story over and over about the accident but never how he got to Ward 13. I try to listen to each and every word to get the story straight. But I can't because Rodney confuses me by rambling and changing the subject over and over. There never seems to be an ending. After nearly an hour of Rodney's ramblings, I decide to leave and rest my swirling head.

On March 25th, my fifth day on the floor, I get "privileges" to leave the floor for a hour. The doctors have given me "off-ward privileges" but are restricted to the hospital grounds. I need some money and ask one of the nurses to open my locker.

She starts yelling at me, "Did you read your handbook, lockers can only be opened at 8:30 p. m." My blood pressure goes up and I yell at her, "That Is Not In The Handbook." Before I get myself in trouble, some other nurse comes over and opens the locker.

Armed with ten ones and some change, I leave the floor on my way to freedom. I rush to get on an elevator and find the vending machines and there are ten different vending machines. I'm in heaven. I get some coffee and hostess chocolate cupcakes. I still have forty-five minutes and decide to go outside and walk the hospital grounds. It feels so good to breath fresh air again and see all the sights life has to give. I'm back at the ward just before my hour is up.

On Saturday March 26, a man is screaming, yelling, but can't talk, like someone in horrible pain. Nurses are running down, back and forth down the hallway into his room. The nurses have looks of sheer panic on their faces. A blonde nurse comes running flat out towards the Nurses Station. She stops because she is breathing so hard and needs to catch her breath to talk. She's panting, and tells the other nurses, "You need you get down here."

Nurses are taking the screaming man's vital signs as they try to get him in a chair. Paging over the network is heard, "Doctor Smith come to Ward 13, Doctor Smith come to Ward 13 - Doctor Smith come to Ward 13."Police show up. They wheel his dead body out. I never felt any panic. *Death is Death.*

Patients are encouraged to shower daily, but some rarely shower, and the smell is very noticeable. If you want a shave, the staff will give you that shave between 8:00 a. m. and 9:00 a. m. Foghorn never took a shower and the stink got to us. We complained to the staff about the stink coming from him and that he had lice in his hair. That day, the staff forced him to take a shower.

Patients are allowed to receive and call out using the two telephones on the left and right corridors. If someone wants to call you, you give them a four-digit extension and the staff will relay a message to you. Calls are limited to 10 minutes but the rule is rarely observed. Many on the floor would always be calling out or receiving calls. I never had any calls.

Patients are allowed visitors from 2:00 p. m. to 8:00 p. m. daily with a restriction of two visitors at one time per patient. Jimmy's father and mother would visit him daily and bring him soda pops and snacks to eat.

On that day, a Nurse came up to me and said, "You've got a visitor. Your wife is here to see you." I'm very surprised to hear that and walk over to the visitor area, but the Nurse has made a mistake. It is Foghorn's wife. She shows up but she does not bring any clothes with her. She is short, not as short as Foghorn, very obese and not very attractive. She is there to serve Foghorn with divorce papers.

It occurred to me that maybe no one knew I am here and that is why I never had any visitors.

Later that night, "The over med man" has flipped out. He is complaining that he has a rash because the doctors are overmedicating him. He starts yelling at a doctor, "My jacket is missing." He is also screaming at a nurse with the doctor, "I want my jacket back." This generates great excitement and huge crowds at Ward 13. Doctors and nurses are running in and out of his room trying to calm him down. There are about 4-5 doctors and 10-15 med students.

He's still yelling, and the call goes into the police. Four huge officers come up and move into his room, push him down to the ground and he is given a shot of Thorazine to calm him down. They put him in restraints. A few hours later he is put on a stretcher and taken off the floor, never to be seen again. I wonder if they did a lobotomy on him.

On March 27, "The Addict" is admitted to the floor. He is a large Black male, around forty years old, built like a linebacker at about 6' 2" and maybe 230 lbs. Word was that he was a former Jailbird who was on the drug program but was caught using heroin again. He is a mean looking guy and not very friendly.

The next morning, as I'm heading up the left corridor towards the dayroom, I hear Jimmy yelling at The Addict, "Stay away from me you're too big for me!" I can hear the fear in Jimmy's voice. He is about to get into a big fight with the addict.

It appears that The Addict was stealing money from people on the floor and Jimmy caught him. The addict denies this. I then hear a chair get thrown by Jimmy and Staff members quickly moving to try and stop things. I try to get in the dayroom so I can get to the right corridor to help Jimmy, but the staff has locked the door.

I ran over to the Nurse Station, but the doors are locked and blocked by staff members. I see The Addict and he looks at me and says, "What are you looking at white boy."

I said, "I'm looking at a thief who stole my money."

That really makes him mad. He says, "I didn't take no one's money."

I said to him, "You're a liar." He yells back at me, and he tries to get through the Nurse's gate, "No one calls me a liar."

I slowly backed into the phone on the wall. If he comes through that gate I'm gonna hit him on the top of his head with all my might with the phone. Hopefully, that might slow him down so I can wrap the phone cord around his neck. Then I will use my secret weapon I have in my pocket; a pen and the point will serve to be a stabbing tool into the deepest parts of his eyes.

Before anything can happen, the Police come, and he is given a shot of Thorazine to calm him down. This was still not enough, and they had to give him a second dose a few hours later and take him off the floor.

On March 28, "The Spy" arrived. He looked twenty-five but said he is thirty-five and was in the Gulf War on a ship. First he said he was married, but later on said he was divorced. I didn't like, nor do I trust this guy.

He comes into the Dining Room around 10PM. It was only him and me. He started the conversation. We talk about PTSD. He said he didn't have anything like that. He said he was in for drug abuse, yet he said he was on no medicine. He had no patient bracelet and appeared to be too clean cut and was still wearing street clothes. I figured he was a spy for the doctors.

Later he leaves saying he had to get a drink of water and returns with Tattoo nurse. He starts talking about how patient I am making a puzzle. Around 10:40PM he says he's going to sleep yet comes back around 10:50Pm and switches channels to a basketball game. He keeps saying he might be leaving on Tuesday. Several times he said to me that the doctors said I wasn't going home. My blood is boiling but I ignore him. I think the doctors are testing me to see if I become violent. I didn't fall for any of their tricks. The Spy left on Tuesday March 29.

My three-day maximum lock-up time turned into ten days. On March 30, 2005, I was released and on my way to a six-month Post traumatic stress disorder (PTSD) treatment program.

I arrived at Building 5 for my Psychosocial Residential Rehabilitation Treatment. I check in and Nurse Kay Mountain wants me to sign some paper to check in.

I tell her, "I can't read the paper because I don't have my reading glasses. I was told that I would have today off to take care of things I need to do."

She keeps saying, "You're not going home." I get agitated and start yelling at her, "I'm not signing anything till I get my day off."

I'm causing quite a scene and they page the psych doctor to come down. Dr. Carmen comes down and gives me a pill to calm me down and says you will get a day off soon, but not today. I finally calm down.

The next day is my physical. I tell the nurses and doctors my problems: Lower back pain, constant swirling sounds and buzzing in my right ear; Pounding headaches that feel like someone is pounding on the right side of my head and my right eye feels like toothpicks are being stuck into my eye.

I'm given a series of tests. First is a hearing test and I was found to have a slight amount of hearing loss in my right ear. They believe the swirling sound in my right ear might be tinnitus.

Tinnitus is the perception of sound when no actual noise is present. It is not a disease but a symptom that can result from a number of underlying causes. In my cause, noise-induced hearing loss that resulted from exposure to loud sounds in Vietnam. [72]

X-Rays are done on my back and CT Scan of my head, and both come back negative, but I am found to be a "borderline diabetic." This starts a huge discussion with me and the old cow, Nurse Widebody. She starts screaming at me, "You either have diabetes or you don't have diabetes. There is no such thing as a "borderline diabetic."

She is starting to piss me off and I can feel my blood pressure going up as I explode on her.

---

[72]   American Tinnitus Association - www. ata. org/understanding-facts

I say to Nurse Widebody, "You don't know what you're talking about. Your own doctor said I'm a borderline diabetic, so therefore I'm a diabetic."

She goes on to say, The doctor is wrong, he used an old test.

I'm thinking that she needs to be on Ward 13, not as a Nurse, but as a patient.

I say to her, "Look you psycho bitch, you need to be committed." She leaves in a huff, and I go to see the doctor who determines that I'm a type 2 diabetic and that it can be controlled by diet with no need for medicine.

Later, I'm told by a doctor that I have racing thoughts and therefore, I'm deemed to be bipolar and put on medicine to control my bipolar and depression.

Bipolar disorder is a brain disorder that is associated with unusual shifts in mood, energy, activity levels and the ability to carry on daily tasks.

After six weeks, I begin my final phase, a six-eight-week program of intensive PTSD training. You are required to live at the hospital with other patients and you must attend daily meetings that last all day from Monday thru Friday. You are off in the evenings and weekends but can't go home for the first week.

My group of eight veterans are all united in our dislike and distrust of our main doctor, Dr. Kevin Shrinkey. In one class, Dr. Shrinkey tries to get me worked up. He keeps pushing me and finally I say, "Move on to the next person".

He keeps pushing me and I finally had enough and say to him, "How would you like me to come over there and choke you to death."

The session is halted, and everyone is dismissed.

CHAPTER 13

Retirement

(2005 to present)

The VA therapist had warned us after treatment to stay away from alcohol and not get involved in any relationships.

By the end of 2005, Social Security had granted my claim for total disability. I'm fifty-eight, divorced, homeless, all alone, and not sure what to do what my life. The first thing I did was find an apartment and sign a one-year lease. The area was surrounded by many bars that were frequented by young college types. I thought I'd be able to communicate with people maybe 30 years younger and that might help me with my image problems.

I enjoyed hanging around the younger crowd but didn't realize how out of place I was until an older man in one of the bars said to me, "Hey, old school". I didn't know at that time but that is how some younger people refer to "old people and old things." I couldn't wait until my lease was up so I could move to another area. The drinking and constant rejections was not helping me.

May 2007 to October 2008 were very lonely times for me. I had just moved and started going to bars near my new apartment. I found one bar that I enjoyed going to 1-2 times a week. It was a decent mix of a younger crowd and twenty-seven and a few "old school" people. Some people were fooled by me and thought me about twenty years younger than I was.

After being rejected by many young ladies, I decided to move to another area. I would travel further South to bars that had some older women, but still too young for me.

I got involved with a group of four women that turned out to be nothing but tramps, liars, and thieves. These women looked for older men in bars. They would start out slowly and then work themselves into your life and find out if you had money. After knowing you for a brief time, the requests to "borrow money" would be worked into the conversation. Three of the four "borrowed money." None ever paid me back anything.

On May 2008, after a four-year struggle, the VA granted me a permanent 100% disability evaluation for my service-connected disabilities, effective May 20, 2004. I was deemed to be disabled because of PTSD with major depression, that markedly interfered with my ability to interact effectively and work efficiently.

The Psychologist who examined me, wrote in her report,

"He reported, that in the two years prior to the current evaluation, he had been diagnosed with diabetes mellitus and hypertension, two concerns which have been linked to traumatic stress by recent research. Considerable paranoia was evident, particularly as related to his nearly constant perception of threat. He demonstrated a history of both suicidal and homicidal ideation. Severe depressive symptoms were apparent, as was severe personality pathology and schizoid personality traits. Symptoms are service-connected and severe. He represents a threat to any work environment. He is incapable of functioning in a normal environment. He is quickly and easily angered and has the capacity for violent behavior.

In June 2008, I was about to turn sixty-one and the snow and cold in Cleveland were getting to me. In September 2008, I left Ohio and bought a new house in North Las Vegas. On my car ride to Las

Vegas, going through Colorado, I hit an open area with no one around me. I pushed the accelerator to the floor. The landscape is wising by as I near the Nevada border. Out of nowhere, on the opposite side of the highway, a police car comes flying by and quickly turns to pursue me.

I have four handguns in my car and fear he will search my car and arrest me. I'm debating killing him if he stops me.

I slow down and hope for the best. He approaches me and says, "I clocked you at 105 MPH. What are you doing going so fast." I say to the officer, "I just bought a home in Las Vegas and I'm anxious to get there. I didn't think I was going so fast."

I hold my breath, hoping he won't search my car.

He says, "I'm gonna give you a speeding ticket, but I won't detain you and you can just plead guilty and pay the fine. But I want you to slow down." I was very thankful and said, "Thank you officer, I will be very careful about my speed." For the rest of the trip, I stayed very close to the speed limit until I got to Las Vegas.

For about 18 months, life was good in Las Vegas. The first year was a fun time for me. I saw and went to four casino grand openings. There was the Aliante, an upscale casino, in North Las Vegas that was very close to my house. Next was the M Resort Spa Casino, a four-star upscale casino on the southern end of the Las Vegas Strip. And finally, two upscale casinos opened on the strip. The Cosmopolitan, with adjacent views of the Bellagio fountains, and the Encore, a AAA Five Diamond Award Winner, on the north side of the strip. New clubs and restaurants were opening everywhere. I had visions of my property doubling in value.

I was gambling almost every day, but just doing OK. However, I did find that game I grew to love, video poker. I loved playing machines for hours. And I got very good at it. I hit around 35 Royal Flushes and four of a kinds in the hundreds on quarter machines.

I was hoping to move up to dollar machines soon. I needed to build up my gambling bankroll. Several things were keeping me from achieving my gambling goals. I was paying $500-$800 a month just to keep up with interest on credit card debt. Over the last few years, while I wasn't working, I had accumulated over $60,000 in credit card debt. Then the housing bubble burst.

My house payment had gone up because of an increase in property taxes, while property values were falling like a rock. The housing market had started to collapse, and Las Vegas was the worst market in the country. I thought I had gotten a great deal on my house when I bought it for $270,000 and had planned to hold for 3-4 years, then sell for a profit of around $100,000. But after being in my house for less than a year, I was shocked to find that it was now worth about $170,000. I did not see any hope for property values to raise for a very long time

Real estate experts thought it might be ten years or longer, before values would return to 2008 values.

I thought of walking away from my loan but knew I couldn't since I had bought it with a VA loan. The VA would quickly take the money every month from my disability check.

There were other things adding to my frustrations. I had also gone through much of my savings on improvements to my house, fixing my teeth, and huge gambling losses in my first year in Las Vegas. I found the people of Las Vegas to be very unfriendly and dating prospects were not going well. The Las Vegas police, a very violent force, seemed out of control.

The weather had been over 100 degrees for nearly six months. The pills the VA had me on were making me exhausted. I found that most days, I was sleeping more and not feeling well. I found out that the two medicines I was taking for depression and bipolar, are called, "Heat Drugs". This was causing my extreme tiredness. I thought it would be easy, I could just go cold turkey.

My first attempt of two weeks went very badly. It felt like my head was going to explode from the pounding. I read about the side effects of the bipolar medicine that could lead to seizures. So I had to wait for the temperature to cool. I got back on the medicines and waited for the temperature to cool. It took me over two months, but I was finally able to get off the "heat drugs."

A week later, I finally got the break I needed. I was playing Texas Hold'em at the M Resort. One of the players was a friend that I called Mike T. I told Mike about my problem. He said he could help me get rid of my house, it wouldn't cost me anything, and I would be able to get out of my VA loan and not owe the government anything.

I asked Mike how he could do all this. Mike said he would do a short sale for me. While Mike was new at these real estate transactions, Mike's partner had over thirty years' experience in real estate in the Las Vegas area. I was very impressed. A few days later, I signed a contract with Mike's real estate company. Now I had a way to sell my house and eventually get out of Las Vegas.

I then decide, like in the Godfather, it was time to take care of some family business.

The next family business to deal was with my credit card companies. Just as soon as my house went up for sale, I quit making any payments to credit card companies. I walked away from $60,000 in debt. I thought these credit card companies had helped to push me further into debt by constantly sending me credit cards and increasing my card limits. For about ninety days, no one from the credit card companies called me. But after that, the hate mail and phone calls began. They would threaten to garnish my wages. I knew they couldn't do it since my disability income was exempt from creditors.

When the threat of garnishment didn't work, they threatened to take my house away. I laughed at that since I was doing a short sale. And the final threat was, "We will take your car away". That made me laugh the most. I said to them, "Go ahead it's a leased car." After about six months, they gave up and wrote the loans off.

Within six months, the short sale went through. My house was sold, and I didn't have to make any house payments during those six months. The house got sold to a veteran who had a nice family. That made me feel much better. The bank and VA let me walk away from the loan. I would suffer some penalty that would take time to heal. My credit would be ruined for about seven years.

Now I needed a place to stay and needed a roommate with good credit to sign the lease with me. I was able to work out a deal that costs me a few extra hundred dollars a month on a nine-month lease. This would help me later so I could get a lease on my own.

On March 2011, I moved to a cheaper apartment close to the strip. I hated the apartment, but the rent was cheap. I signed a one-year lease and decided that I would leave Las Vegas for good at the end of March 2012 and go back to Ohio.

My lease was up on my car, and I went to Honda because they said they would give me a "customer loyalty" discount.

Since I was getting off the drugs, I wasn't thinking that clearly.

They took advantage of me and sold me a car at retail with super high interest rates. They said that since my credit was so bad, that was the best deal possible. The dealership said to sign the papers and they would see if they could get me approved. I signed the papers.

The next day, I noticed a small dent on the new car and decided to take the car back. When I got there, my salesperson was nowhere to be found. They all said I had to talk with him. I told them I didn't want the car. They ignored me. I called Honda "customer service" and they gave me the run around and said I had to deal with that dealership.

I waited a few months and drove the car without making any payments. I was going to do that if I could. But along the way, my insurance on the car had lapsed and I couldn't get any coverage on the car. I called Honda and told them I was giving the car back and would not make any more payments. They quickly came and towed the car away. Within a month, I got a bill for around $7000. They said they had to sell that new car as an old car at auction and that was what I owed them. I told them to go to hell and that I would never buy anything for them ever again. My credit was already bad, so another bill didn't matter.

Very quickly, my credit score, which had been 775 when I moved to Las Vegas, was down to 350. For six months, I had to ride buses to get around and I cut way back on my gambling. Within six months, I was able to save $9000 and pay cash for a 2005 Buick Lacrosse with very low mileage. I now had a reliable car that would get me home. I started saving all I could for my return home to Ohio.

My apartment was within walking distance of three casinos. The people that lived in apartments in this area were all locals, mostly lower-middle class. Most of the tenants worked at casinos. There was lots of retired people who seemed to be living from paycheck-to-paycheck and for the comps they received monthly from the surrounding casinos. Many of the tenants were prostitutes, drug dealers, drug users, and near homeless people. A bunch of "undesirables", however, I found some of the tenants to be very interesting.

Even though rent was cheap, the apartment complex had an outdoor swimming pool, a spa, and a nice workout room. The apartment complex would celebrate all the typical holidays and the non-typical holidays like Valentine's Day, Easter, and Halloween. They would decorate the office and the staff would wear outfits to match the holiday. That helped to make you feel part of a community, which was nice.

The apartment manager, Betty, was an older woman in her seventies. She lived in one of the apartments with her husband. She was a big smoker, and you could always find a cigarette in her hand. She would cough as she puffed and put more of the toxic smoke into her lungs. Her face had the look of an old gray rhino. It was old and wrinkled due to many years of smoking. I hate to think what her lungs look like.

I would go swimming in the middle of the day when very few were at the pool. Since it would get very hot in the summer months,

I would only stay for one to two hours during that time frame. Every day, I would see the same guy at the pool. He would be tanning various parts of his body. He would lay in the super-hot sun, day after day, for hours, his head always covered with a towel. He was always there before me and after I left.

One day, he came over and introduced himself as Bob Zemsoski, or something close to that spelling. He was a large Polish man, sixty and divorced. He came to Las Vegas from Detroit about five years ago and lived month-to-month off half of his pension from General Motors. The other half of his pension went to his ex-wife.

He was always borrowing money from those loan shark places that would charge him over twenty-five percent interest rates. He talked about a movie script he has written and how Hollywood would discover him someday and he would be rich. But until that time, Bob would go to dumpsters and get day old food like chips, cookies, candies that owners of vending machines had thrown out because they were past the expiration dates. Since Bob was from Detroit, I called him "Detroit Bob." We hit it off very well and became very good friends.

One day, one of Bob's buddies, Randy, was at the pool. He was a silver-haired man in his sixties and had come to Las Vegas several years ago from the Chicago area. He was a retired fireman and had, over the years, won several lawsuits while in Las Vegas. He seemed to be involved in many "accidents" over the years. Because of that, I nicknamed him, "Sue them Randy." He was a good guy with a big heart. He was also an excellent video poker player. His problem was that he liked to drink and take drugs while playing poker machines. This was a bad combination and he lost thousands of dollars. When I last saw Randy, he was running low on money and hoping to hit it big on the machines or maybe be involved in another "accident."

I lived upstairs in a two-story building near the swimming pool. My downstairs neighbor was a crazy old white man in his sixties. He was always complaining to the office about all the noise I made, which was not true since I was rarely home. I called him "The angry Russian Hermit."

He rarely ever left his apartment. I don't believe he even had a job. Sometimes at night he would leave for a few hours but was always back before nightfall. He drove some awful looking old red car that must have had over a million miles on it. Management finally tired of his complaining and told him to leave if he did not like living in the complex. I found out he had been living at the complex for nearly ten years and had complained about previous neighbors before me. I pity the next person that must live above him.

Just directly across from me, in another building, lived "Corvette Sally." She was an older white woman in her seventies who walked with a limp and used a cane to help steady herself. So, I was surprised to see her get into a mint 1967 Corvette and zoom down the street. She had bought the Corvette in 1967 when it was brand new. She told me she had offers up to $40,000 for the car but would never sell it. I found out from Detroit Bob that her husband had died quite a few years ago and left her very well off. Many times, I would see her at the casino gambling.

Many days when I was walking around the apartment complex, I would see "the old man and his son." They both lived in the complex in the old man's apartment. The son was about fifty. A liar who didn't work. He was going to school to learn about computers and getting money from the government. Bob said he had been going to school for over ten years. The son lived with his father, an old man about eighty, who always walked with a walker. The son and old man lived off the meager social security. The son was a big smoker and always trying to "borrow" smokes from anyone that would give him one. Many of the guys in the complex did not like or trust the son. Bob said he had "borrowed" money from Randy, many months ago, and had still not given him back the money.

Bob lived a few buildings down me and I would visit him often. Bob's apartment was full of things that others who had moved out of the complex would leave on the curb. Bob had about ten different televisions he had collected. They would be across a shelf, one on top of another and all on different channels. Bob was a big hockey fan and many of the stations were on hockey games.

Bob always had someone visiting him. Homeless Greg would visit often. He was a young white man about thirty. He and his brother lived from paycheck to paycheck. Their only means of transportation was a lone bicycle and only means of income came from blood banks where they would sell their blood. You could see the visible holes on their arms where blood had been drawn for a period of nearly ten years.

Another odd person was this overweight white man, about thirty-five. He lived with his mother and depended on her for all his income. He was heavy into drugs. I'm pretty sure his mother did not know about his drug habit. He wore braces and had this nasty habit of "clicking" his teeth, so I called him "The Clicker."

The drugs would come from Bob's next-door neighbor, "Debbie the drug dealer." Debbie was a fifty plus white woman who may have been attractive about twenty years ago; however, no one had told her lately. She still thought she was "hot." Debbie was another who lived paycheck to paycheck. Her only source of income was supplying drugs to the tenants in the complex. Her problem was that she used drugs and was a terrible gambler. She had the odd living arrangement of living with her current boyfriend and her ex-husband in the same apartment.

One day Bob and I went over to the Palm's casino to place a bet at the sports book. Randy was there and drinking with his friend, "Buzz the Horse Man." Buzz was around sixty-five. He dressed very well and gave you the impression that he was an astute businessman who had a nice income, however, none of that was true. Buzz was a hard drinker, a coke addict, a liar, and a huge passion for betting on the horses. Buzz was a man given to visions of grandeur and lying. He would brag to people that he was well off and had been an owner of a million-dollar bar. None of that was true. He lived in a worn-down apartment, did not own a car, had no job, and had been fired from that bar for stealing money from his employer.

Every Sunday, this older, very thin woman, around sixty, would visit the dumpsters in the area. It was usually very early in the morning, and I would watch her from my apartment window. She would crawl inside this huge dumpster to retrieve aluminum cans and any other types of items she might be able to sell. She always wore the same dirty clothes. She never had a mask or gloves on. I called her "The dirty dumpster woman."

For my last two months in Las Vegas, I was planning on increasing my gambling budget to $1,000 a month, hoping to maybe win a few thousand dollars before I left. However, on Friday, February 3, 2012, my world came to abrupt halt. I woke up that morning with a terrible back pain. It was a very sharp pain, and I was having trouble breathing. I thought maybe I had a pulled muscle and started taking Advil, hoping that might help. I would take more Advil every four hours, but the pills did no good.

I was now worried that I might be having a heart attack. The pain kept getting worse and I couldn't take it anymore. By now, it was nearly midnight. I got in my car and drove to the VA hospital. I checked into the Emergency room and waited nearly two hours before I was admitted. Since I had said that I might be having a heart attack, the nurses and doctors treated me as if I was having a heart attack. They performed various tests and determined I was not having a heart attack, but still didn't know what was causing the pain.

The pain was getting much worse. It was a ten out of ten pain. it felt like someone had hit me on my back with a hammer and broke all my bones. It was the worst pain I had ever been in. I kept asking for pain medicine. It would take nearly ten hours before I was given morphine for the pain. That helped for a few hours. But the pain was back.

I couldn't sleep in the bed. I sat in a chair and tried to sleep but couldn't sleep much. On Saturday, they started me on a pain medicine that only helped for about 45 minutes. The problem was the medicine could only be taken every four hours, so I would be in pain for more than three hours till my next dose would arrive.

It took two days, but by Sunday morning, Dr. Brown had the answer to my problem. The hospital had taken blood test and determined I had tested positive for pansenstive staph aureus. In other words, bacteria had gotten into my blood stream. I was put on iv antibiotics. After a three day stay, I was discharged from the hospital.

After being on antibiotics for 14 days, I was taken off them on February 19, 2012. I kept telling the doctors I was still in horrible pain. The pain killers they had given me were not working. However, they concluded that it appeared unlikely because of the negative blood cultures. Therefore, they decided, "There is no need for more antibiotics."

Dr. Brown had told he was concerned that the blood infection could spread to my bones.

On February 21, 2012, my primary doctor had requested an MRI on my Cervical Spine since X-Rays are not the best for detecting possible problems. However, no urgency was attached to the order and the MRI was not conducted until March 13, 2012. On March 14, 2012, after having gotten results of the MRI, my primary doctor called me and said to go to the Emergency Room immediately. The bacteria had spread to my bones and had been eating away at my spine all this time. This was at the top of my neck area and now about six inches of neck spine were gone.

I went immediately to the Emergency Room and was quickly transferred to University Medical Las Vegas. After all this time had passed, I was now advised to wear an Aspen Collar "to immobilize my spine to prevent any worsening injury." The Aspen Collar is basically a neck brace. It is very rigid with very little give. It covers all of your neck and part of your chin. I found this collar to be very uncomfortable and impossible to sleep with it on. On March 18, 2012, I was placed on antibiotics again. This time they were treating me as having osteomyelitis.

An infection and inflammation of the bone or bone marrow.

They wanted to do the operation at this Las Vegas hospital, but since they had a bad reputation, I refused. I was only two weeks away from going home to Ohio and knew I would never let any hospital in Las Vegas operate on me. I would go back and have the operation in Ohio. I did not want to die in Las Vegas. The Las Vegas hospital was dead set against me leaving and driving. They said, if someone hit me, my spine could collapse, and I would die.

I left Las Vegas at the end of March 2012. It was a long grueling drive back to Ohio. It took about three days. I would drive about 800 miles per day. Several times I almost fell asleep at the wheel.

On April 7 I checked into the VA hospital in Cleveland. A few days later, I was transferred to University Hospital. They performed the nearly seven-hour surgery on Friday, April 13, 2012.

I'm waking up from a deep sleep. Things are out of focus. I see people and hear muted voices. I feel a tube in my throat. I start to panic. I'm lying flat on a hospital bed, can't talk or move. I'm thinking, "Did the operation go terribly wrong? I'm I a vegetable?"

I see a nurse running towards me. I'm making frantic motions with my hand in a writing motion. She senses I want to communicate with her and says, "Hold on, I'll get some paper and a pen." She's back in a few minutes. I struggle to write, "I can't feel anything, did the operation go bad?" She says everything is OK. Then I try to pull the tube out of my throat, and she stops me and says "Hold on. I'll get a doctor to take it out." It's so uncomfortable. It's like being under water and you can't breathe.

Finally, three days later, it was about thirty minutes later, the doctor showed up. After the tube came out, I kept telling the nurses I was going to throw up. I said, "Get me a pan", they kept on ignoring me until I threw up all over the bed I was on.

I stayed at the University Hospital until April 25, 2012, and transferred back to the Cleveland VA hospital, where I was finally discharged on May 1, 2012. On October 8, 2013, I met with Pain Mismanagement about follow up X-Rays on my neck.

The doctor says, "This was a very serious operation. You're extremely lucky. With C2-C7 fusion, many die from that operation.

You will never improve, but you can expect that you will get used to it. The operation was very close to the brain. A threat of Infection to your hardware can be very dangerous so you probably will have to stay on antibiotic medicine for the rest of your life."

I'm now held together with a bunch of screws. My movement is very restricted. I can't turn or bend like a normal person. I blame the VA and their lousy hospitals for letting this infection spread and not being able to treat me in a timely fashion. The VA took nearly two months to understand the problem and failed to treat me properly.

Up until 2012, I was in good physical health. But since then, my body has started to breakdown. In addition to my neck problems, my left leg, where the bone was taken for the operation, is still numb in areas. It feels like blood is restricted from flowing. The bottom of my left foot feels swollen. After many years of complaining to the VA, they performed some tests on my left leg. They found that I have nerve damage that was likely caused by the surgery.

I also have been complaining to the VA about my right shoulder for over three years. Sometime around June 2013, they took an X-Ray. Two different doctors said I have Arthritis, and nothing can be done to help me. I kept telling them it was more than Arthritis, and I want a second opinion. They refused my request.

Around December 2014, I complained to the Director of Patient Care at the Cleveland VA. He set up a consult to see my primary doctor. I then got to see a rheumatology doctor on Friday, February 13, 2015. After she examined me, she thought I might have 1-2 torn ligaments in my right shoulder. She had me do a second X-Ray that day.

On March 2, 2015, I was given an MRI. Two days later, the results confirmed that I had two torn ligaments. On April 2, 2015, I had a consul with Orthopedics to determine what they can do for me. The VA doctor from Orthopedics, confirmed that I have a Rotator Cuff tear in my right shoulder.

He said, "I have bad news for you. There is a very low chance of a successful operation to repair that tear. You don't have enough muscle in that area and have found that others like that don't have successful operations. Maybe in a few years, you might be able to get a shoulder replacement."

I was very disappointed to hear that.

I've been trying to improve my physical health by walking, to strengthen my legs, and neck exercises to expand my range of motion. My daily routine consists of forcing myself to walk three miles daily. I experience constant neck pain, tire easily, and must sit most of the day with my back against something. I can't lift much weight, play slots for any period longer than thirty minutes, or play any sports.

On May 29, 2010, Ed Burke, my company commander from Charlie Company died. He had Cancer and let it go until it was at stage 3 and then it was too late. I believe many Vietnam Veterans are dying from suicide, accidents, and cancer, diabetes, and heart disease that is directly linked to Agent Orange and other chemicals sprayed in Vietnam.

In 2009, of the 2,709,918 Americans who served in Vietnam, less than 850,000 are estimated to still be alive. [73]

---

73   *Source: The VFW Magazine, the Public Information Office, and HQ CP Forward Observer &* blogs. ancestry. com/ancestry/2014/11/10/remembering-and-researching-vietnam-era-veterans

EPILOGUE

No American soldier has ever suffered the level of disrespect from the American people, than the men who fought in the Vietnam War.

Jane Fonda, dubbed, "Hanoi Jane", voiced her opposition to the Vietnam War by traveling to Hanoi, North Vietnam, in July 1972. She posed for a photo wearing an enemy helmet, seated on a North Vietnamese anti-aircraft battery that was used to shoot down American pilots.

Just a few hundred yards away, American POWs were being tortured at the Hoa Lo Prison, more commonly known as the "Hanoi Hilton." [74]

The "Hanoi Hilton" was a forbidding fortress. Surrounded by thick concrete walls, 15 to 20 feet high, guard towers that ringed the exterior walls, topped by several strands of electrified barbed wire, and jagged glass shards of old French champagne bottles.

The POWs diet was almost exclusively of uncooked and contaminated rice. They slept on bamboo floors without any covering. Starving and exhausted, they were jammed under floors of huts in offal, denied medicine, soap, and adequate food for weeks.

Some were left naked in their own filth, enduring hundreds of mosquito bites, before passing into a coma. Some were punched with

---

74   The Patriot Post, Traitor: "Hanoi Jane" Fonda, http://patriotpost. us/ page/80

clenched fists until they broke several teeth, shattered their nose, and caused their eyelids to swell shut. During the "rope torture", prisoners were forced face down on bunks, ankles set into stocks, and bound tightly with rope at the elbows. Then the long end of the rope was pulled through a hook attached to the ceiling, shoulders seemingly being torn from their sockets, that constricted breathing as they screamed in pain. Others had broken legs twisted, forced to sit or kneel for long periods without food or water. Others were beaten with fan belt-like whips and rifle butts. [75]

Protesters believed they were right and could do as they pleased and break any law. They had no respect for law and contempt for our institutions. They went from mild acts of disobedience; sit-ins, burning draft cards, impeding the registration process, to more radical actions; destroying property, violent confrontations, or fleeing to Canada to avoid the draft. [76]

Abbot Howard Hoffman, one of the leaders in the American Anti-Vietnam movement, expressed the arrogance of the protesters:

"We Were Young. We were Reckless, Arrogant, headstrong - And we were right. I regret nothing." [77]

Hoffman, a manic-depressive, committed suicide shortly after he made his statement.

Since my return from Vietnam, I have suffered from type 2 diabetes, depression, bipolar disorder, Agent Orange exposure, anger issues, alcoholism, drug addiction, anxiety, insomnia, paranoia, violent behavior, severe headaches, nightmares, hearing loss, tinnitus, flashbacks, and survivor guilt. I did not however know that I was suffering from Dissociative Amnesia.

---

75   Rochester, Stewart and Kiley, Frederick, Honor Bound: American Prisoners of War in Southeast Asia 1961-1973

76   Anti-War Protesters Don't End Wars, They Prolong Them, http://www. examier. com/articles/anti-war-protestors-don-t-end-wars-they-prolong-them

77   The Movement of the Sixties: Protests in America from Greensboro to Wounded Knee

Dissociative Amnesia is a mental illness that occurs when a person blocks out certain information, usually associated with a stressful or traumatic event, that leaves them unable to remember important personal information. The memories still exist but are deeply buried within the person's mind and cannot be recalled. [78]

Parts of Vietnam are buried or wiped away from my memories. Many events had been blocked out or distorted from reality. Only when I started getting involved with trying to solve the mystery of October 17, 1967, did I begin to unravel some buried memories:

In 1994, at my second reunion in Las Vegas, Art Cordova, who was with me on April 16, 1967, when Willis was killed. I only remembered the small bullet hole on the front of his body, not many other things that Art remembered. Chris Ronnau remembered me wrapping his wound, but then he told me other things I didn't remember and how I saved his life.

In 2000, I saw an ad from a nephew of Pasquale Tizzio. He was asking if anyone knew his uncle who was killed at the battle of Ong Thanh on October 17, 1967. When I came to Tizzio's name, I stopped and thought, "I was with him in 1967 with 2/28th Charlie company". I came across a photo that I thought was Tizzio. I was 99% sure it was him but needed verification. I sent the photo to the nephew and his father confirmed it was Tizzio. I went back through my photos and found I had the negative of the photo. That meant I had taken the photo. Then some things started to come back to me. There was our conversation in 1967 about becoming the Battalion RTO. It must of been a huge guilt on my part that kept me from remembering my good friend.

In 2002, I saw Frank McMeel again for the first time since 1967. Frank had been Gerald Thompson's RTO in our squad. I was telling Frank the story about when we were on the guard tower on December 26, 1967. That we were part of a guard unit to keep Bob Hope safe

---

78   Web MD, "Mental Health and Dissociative Amnesia", www. webmd. com/
mental-health/associative-amnesia#1

while he came to LaiKhe for his Christmas show. And that Frank was reading me a letter from his mother. Frank then said something to me that startled me. He said he was badly wounded on October 17, 1967, and never returned to the field after that, so it could not of been him.

A few years later, I was able to get in contact with David Laub. He was in 3rd platoon with me in Delta company and knew just about everyone I knew. He had sent me his photo album of pictures he had of Delta company. I wasn't sure who George Smith was and had confused him with Luther Smith who was killed on October 17, 1967. After seeing pictures of George Smith and Luther Smith, I was able to remember George Smith from when I was at Fort Polk, Louisiana. He also had a picture of Kenneth Wilson that I swore was Ronney Reece. But David reminded me that Wilson was with us in Charlie company and had transferred with us to Delta company.

Gerald Thompson had many pictures of our squad from Delta company. He had one picture that someone identified as Ronney Reece. I could remember nothing about his face or mannerisms. In another picture, six of us from my squad, I was able to figure out two other mysteries. I was able to identify five of us. Three in the back row were of Frank McMeel, Donnie Hodges, and Reynolds Lonefight. The three of them had survived the battle on October 17, 1967. In the front row was myself, Gary Lincoln, killed on October 17, 1967, and another soldier next to me that I wasn't sure who he was but knew I had to know him very well. I found that I had several other photos of this mystery soldier. After some process of elimination, I got down to the name of Emil Megiveron. Now I had to verify I had the correct soldier. Emil had been killed on October 17, 1967.

It took some time, but I was able to locate his sister Mary in Michigan. I sent her several photos and she confirmed that was Emil. I was so frustrated since I couldn't remember him. She sent me many letters and photos telling me about Emil, but I couldn't remember anything. I did remember when I went to the hospital after Japan, seeing what I thought was him, but it was Griego. I must of buried that trauma deep within my head.

Mike Troyer, who survived the battle of Ong Thanh, died on January 15, 2019, of a blood clot.

On a Saturday evening, September 1992, I got a very surprised phone call from Mrs. Betty Bolen. It had been almost six years since I first wrote to her in September 1986 about her son Jackie, killed in action on October 17, 1967.

In 1986, Mrs. Bolen was too heartbroken to talk about her son, but on this evening in 1992, she talked to me for over an hour about her Jackie. It was one of my proudest moments to know I had helped this mother. I was determined to try and help many others.

In 1993, I created a Black Lion tradition of having reunions in Las Vegas around the October 17 time frame.

On January 2000, I received an email from David Maraniss, associate editor at the Washington Post. He had seen and read, my writings on the Black Lion website and was especially interested on my writings about the battle on October 17, 1967. David had a contract with Simon and Schuster for his new book on Vietnam and the sixties. It was scheduled to be published in the fall of 2003. The book was to be about two days in October 1967 to try and explain that era. The Vietnam half of the book would be entirely about the battle of Ong Thanh and the Black Lions who were in the battle.

David wanted to hear from anybody who had been in the battle or knew men who had been in the battle. He was interested in interviewing survivors of the battle and others who were in those companies. He was also interested in any letters or diaries or other mementoes that families had from men who were in the battle.

David said there was a certain coincidence to the story about one of the men killed in that battle, Major Donald Holleder. He was a character in his Vince Lombardi book. Holleder had been a star football player at West Point when Vince Lombardi was the assistant coach.

I was able to contact the Tizzio family and visited them in New York. They couldn't make this reunion but were planning on attending the next reunion in 2002. At the end of 2002, I had located Gerald Thompson and visited him in Tennessee. He had many pictures of the guys from 1967, to include many from our squad.

I was also able to meet with Frank McMeel again. He was badly wounded on October 17, 1967. I also meet the fiancée of Clifford Breeden, point man for Alpha company, who was the first person killed in the battle on October 17, 1967. And I reunited with Gilbert Pizano again. He was in my squad in late October 1967.

Gilbert Pizano passed away on December 12, 2007.

David Maraniss's book "They Marched into Sunlight", came out in 2003, was a finalist for the Pulitzer Prize for History in 2004, won the J. Anthony Lukas book prize, and Tom Hanks bought the rights to make it into a movie.

In October 2003, I received an email from Robert Tilton, the former police chief in Stow. Tilton had just read "They Marched into Sunlight" that had mentioned me being from Stow, Ohio. He had been with the 1st Infantry Division on his way to LaiKhe when the battle had erupted. He told me about how the 1st Infantry Division had quickly started to hush the story about that being an ambush.

The year 2004 was a very eventful year. Earlier in the year, I heard from Robert Kenner Films. They were working on a documentary film based on the book, "They Marched into Sunlight". I gave him some of the survivors contact information.

At the beginning of 2004, Tizzio's sister told me of a conversation she had with Paul Scott. Tizzio had told Paul that if he was killed in Vietnam, he wanted to be buried at Arlington National Cemetery. Tizzio's sister started working on plans to move her brother's body from New York to Arlington National Cemetery. On November 18, 2004, Pasquale Tizzio was buried at Arlington National Cemetery.

Two close friends of the Tizzio family from a funeral home in New York, had driven all night to bring Tizzio to his final resting place. Tizzio was given a full military ceremony and was buried on a nice site that overlooks the Pentagon.

Paul Scott was tragically killed on October 3, 2017. A pickup truck ran a red light and hit Paul's motorcycle broadside. He was killed instantly.

I held another Black Lion reunion in October 2004 at the Sahara in Las Vegas. Robert Kenner Films was filming inside the Presidential Suite. They interviewed many of the survivors who attended the reunion. One of those survivors, was 1st Sgt Clarence "Bud" Barrow, wounded while with Delta company. It was his first reunion, and it took quite a lot of convincing to get him to attend the reunion in Las Vegas.

1st Sgt Barrow passed away on April 29, 2004.

On October 17, 2005, Robert Kenner Films, released their documentary film, "Two Days In October", aired on pbs. org under the American Experience. The film was about the battle of Ong Thanh and the protests at the University of Wisconsin-Madison during the Vietnam War from October 16 to October 17, 1967.

The first half of the film follows the ambush in Vietnam that produces a constant stream of emotional recollections. The second half of the film was about the protestors in Wisconsin that marks the first time a antiwar protest turned violent. The film was very well received and won a Peabody Award in 2005.

In February 2006, Susan Katz Keating, wrote an article about the battle of October 17, 1967, that appeared in the Veterans of Foreign Wars magazine (VFW), pages 34-36. The article was titled, "Black Lions, Battle of Ong Thanh."

On August 26, 2006, Random House published "Blood Trails" by Chris Ronnau. I was with Chris in Vietnam and helped patch him up on the day he was wounded in April 1967. The book was based on the journal Chris kept while in Vietnam that gives you a real perspective on the everyday life of a combat infantry soldier in Vietnam.

Chris Ronnau passed away on June 14, 2015, and was buried at Arlington National Cemetery.

On April 1, 2013, FX announced on Deadline Hollywood, they had put into development, "They Marched into Sunlight", a six-part limited TV series. The project will be based on the bestseller by David Maraniss.

Vietnam certainly changed my life and those around me. Our group of six from my childhood were very close growing up, but after Vietnam, we all split up and went through many changes.

After his discharge, Ray started work in Jacksonville, Florida as a machine apprentice. He found the job not what he wanted and came home to Ohio for what he thought was a waiting job. The job offer didn't materialize and for a few months, Ray was homeless. He got a break in life when his fiancé's mother took him into their home. Within a year they were married, and Ray got a job at the post office as a letter carrier. During the years, they had three children and Ray retired from the post office.

John got married, had three children, and later divorced. He worked at the same job for nearly fifty years and retired. He was in excellent health until age 68, but then emergency heart surgery changed his life. He has some trouble getting around but enjoying life with his children and grandchildren.

When I met with Denny in 2006, I asked him about Geno and was surprised to hear he had not been in contact with him since 1972. When I came back from Vietnam, they were very close as they were both involved with heavy drug use. Denny said he heard he was still living in the area, but that no one he knew had heard from him.

I started to think maybe Geno had passed away and was determined to find him and see how life had treated him all these years. It would not be easy to find him because he changed his last name to a very common last name after his return from Vietnam. It took all my private investigator training to locate Geno after many failed attempts.

I found out that he keeps to himself, has been married nearly forty years, and has three children and lives close to me. It was a friendly chat on the phone with a promise from him to meet sometime soon, however, I felt there was more to the story. It's been over two years since that phone call. I have left several messages but no returned calls. I think he is having many demons to deal with, that may include drug use from his constant physical and mental pain.

By 1979, Billy was getting his life together and was able to fulfill his dream of owning his own bar. He bought a bar and named it, The Deer Hunter Lounge, after his favorite movie, The Deer Hunter. But bad luck followed Billy, and several months later, he killed a man in the bar who lunged at him with a knife. The killing was ruled to be justifiable since Billy acted in self-defense.

I didn't see Billy again till 2005 when he attended Ray's youngest daughter's wedding. He was getting help from the VA for his PTSD problems and was very happy in his life. He had bought a house in Nevada and was getting ready to move.

Billy was killed in a car accident in 2006. He had just moved to Reno, Nevada and was enjoying his life. Some women had a heart attack while driving, crossed over into the other side of the highway and hit Billy head on. He died instantly. When Billy got married in 1971, he invited me to the wedding, and I never went. That really upset him, so I wanted to make it up to him. Ray, his brother Joe, and I attended his funeral.

In 2006, from out of nowhere, Denny's sister contacted my sister and said Denny wanted me to contact him. Since I had not seen or heard from Denny since 1972, I was more than eager to contact him. But it wasn't exactly what I was hoping for. Denny had contracted a rare blood disorder and was planning for his death that could happen at any time. During the long three-hour drive to his home, I thought back to the good times when we were younger.

Over the years, I heard many rumors about Denny, so I was looking forward to separating fact from fiction. It was a stunning transformation when I saw Denny again. He looked many years older than his biological age of 56. He looked much thinner than I remembered, like he had been up for many days without sleep. But it was his skin that really shook me. His once beautiful light-colored skin was discolored. His arms and legs had ugly scaly crusty spots that were a mix of purple and red patches and raised sores.

But the one thing that had not changed; he still had that great personality filled with wit and humor. We talked for hours. He told me about the blood disease that was killing him slowly. He had married in the late 1970s to the love of his life. But the person that he was so proud of was his only daughter. He said he loved her so much and will miss her very much. When I left, it was with a heavy heart knowing Denny would be gone soon. Denny passed away on January 14, 2007, from a blood disease. The blood disease was likely caused by his exposure to Agent Orange in Vietnam in 1967.

Drinking and drugs dulled my mind, and I repressed many things. After many years, some of the memories began to reappear. One of them was Annie G. I never wrote to her while I was in Vietnam, but after fifty years I wanted to find her and see how her life had turned out.

I was having a hard time finding her, but after many months, my private detective training played off and I found her. But the results were not what I had hoped for. After sending her a letter, I was looking forward to hearing her voice again and talking about old times. Instead, I got a call from the police department where she lives. She had reported me to them and said I was scaring her since she barely remembered me.

The police said she wanted me to leave her alone. I was very disappointed to hear that since I thought she would be thrilled to hear from me again. I told the police that I wished her no ill will, explained why I had contacted her, and that I would not contact her again. The next day, I got an email from her and she took a very defensive tone in her email.

She said she didn't remember the note and was suspicious of me after waiting fifty years to contact her. We exchanged a few other emails, and she went from nice to defensive to nice again. I did learn from her that she had moved out of the neighborhood while I was in the Army. After graduating from high school, she married a returning Vietnam Veteran in 1971. He was in an infantry unit and was wounded in action. On his return from Vietnam, he had severe PTSD and started drinking trying to forget what he saw in Vietnam.

Less than a year into their relationship, her husband started verbally and physically abusing her. He started with pushing her and that quickly escalated into sexual abuse of her and her two children. The marriage ended in divorce in 1978 over his abuse and PTSD issues. He died in 2007 after suffering from cancer likely caused by his exposure to Agent Orange.

Annie married again in 1983, but that marriage also ended in divorce. She has gained a lot of weight, has health issues, and is very unhappy in her life. The emails probably left both of us unfilled. She wanted to know more about the note but refused to talk about the past that I so desperately wanted to talk about.

The problems started slowly in 2003 with forgetfulness and confusion like not recognizing where home is and calling family members by other names. By early 2004, loved ones were perceived in new and usual ways, being accused of theft and other improper behavior.

By the end of 2004, the problems got much worse as my mother was wandering from home and leaving the oven on. At this point, it was no longer safe to leave her alone. Doctors did a medical examination and determined my mother had dementia. A few weeks later, my sister had to put her into a nursing home.

Dementia is a general term for a decline in mental ability severe enough to interfere with daily life.

Ten years later, at the end of February 2014, the nursing home informed us that our mother was no longer eating and could no longer talk and had less than two weeks to live.

On the morning of March 5, 2014, my two brothers, sister, and I were at her bedside during her last hours. I think that made her very happy. My siblings left for a few minutes, and I was alone with my mother.

I said to her, "You will be seeing the old man soon", referring to my father, and that didn't get much of a reaction from her. Then I said to her, "You will also see Tony again", referring to my stepfather, and that brought a small smile to her face and a sparkle to her eyes. Less than an hour later, on March 5, 2014, my mother passed away at age 90.

With her passing, I was taken back to those early summers as a teenager. My mother and Tony would play and sing Mexican songs all weekend long. My stepfather was born in Mexico, and I grew to love that music.

My favorite song is Cielito Lindo, also known as the "Ay, Ay, Ay, Ay song", one of Mexico's most beloved folk songs. This song is commonly played by Mariachi bands and takes me back to happy and sad times, as I remember my mother and stepfather. I am very proud of my Hispanic heritage. Viva Mexico!

I regret the many bad decisions I've made in my life and wish I could redo many things. Spine surgery has slowed me down greatly, but I still hope to travel across the country, maybe in 2020, to meet with other families and friends. As for my personal life, I bought a condo and live alone. There are no women in my life and maybe never will. I stay in constant contact with the loves of my life, my two daughters.

Author's Note

This work is a memoir that reflects my recollections over a period of many years. Certain named individuals and events are of my own creation to protect identities. While I took some literary license in telling my story, the essence of the story is fact based.

No portion of this manuscript may be reproduced in any form without the written permission of the author.

Appendix A

Statistical Summary of The Battle of Ong Thanh

Men Involved: 156   Medals Awarded: 221

Unit/Men Involved	KIA	WIA	Not WIA	MOH	DSC	SS	BS	Arcom	PH
Alpha/65 men	22	33	10			4	37	1	55
Delta/81 men	27	38	16	1	1	7	34	1	65
HHC /10 men	10				2		2		10
(HHC includes Major Holleder)									
* Other						1			
Totals: 156	59	71	26	1	3	12	73	2	130

Notes:

1. Harold "Pinky" Durham was awarded the Medal of Honor

2. Major Holleder was awarded the Silver Star that was later upgraded to the DSC

3. Bill McGath was nominated for a DSC, but never received any medal

4. Clark Welch was nominated for a MOH, but was downgraded to a DSC

5. Fifteen men received No medals of any kind: (7 from Delta; 8 from Alpha)

6. Total Purple Hearts awarded was 130 (71 WIA plus 59 KIA), but many were wounded multiple times

7. * Originally 13 Silver Stars were awarded. Holleder was upgraded to the DSC, the "other" was awarded to Major General Hay, Commanding General of the 1st Infantry Div

8. The location of the battle was in the Province of Binh Long, Military Region 3 (III Corps), UTM Grid of XT685575

9. Six other soldiers were killed on October 17, 1967 in the Province of Binh Long, They were not part of the Battle of Ong Thanh: Willie Goree, 25th Inf Div. ; Christopher Herderick, 25th Inf Div. ; Raymond Minus, 25th Inf Div; Antonio Morales Jr, Armor Intelligence Specialist; Harry Sarsfield, Co C 2nd BN, 2nd Infantry, 1st Inf Div; Anthony Vaickus, 25th Inf Div

10. Joseph Booker died October 18, 1867; Archie Porter died October 21, 1967

Willic C. Johnson died November 9, 1967; Paul Fitzgerald & Olin Hargrove were listed as MIA on October 17, 1967, but were changed to KIA on March 20, 1978

Appendix B

Unit History of 2nd Battalion 28th Infantry

Motto: Vincit Amor Patriae "Love of Country Conquers"

Nickname: "Lions of Cantigny"

Activation: 10 June 1901

Campaigns: Philippine Insurrection: Mindanao

World War I : Lorraine 1917-18, Picardy, Montidier-Noyon, Aisne-Marne,

St. Mihiel, and Meuse-Argonne

World War II: Normandy, Northern France, Rhineland, and Central Europe

Vietnam: Bright Star, Abilene, Brunswick, Silver-City, Bismarck, Los Angles,

Coco Beach, Bowie, Omega, Birmingham, El Paso I & II, Amarillo,

Broome, Lam Son II, Cheyenne, Danbury, Montgomery, Tulsa, Shenandoah I & II, Battle Creek, Attleboro II, Cedar Falls, Tucson, Junction City, Yorktown, Manhattan, Dallas, Bluefield, Rochester, Billings.

The 2nd Battalion, 28th Infantry's lineage starts on 10 June 1901 with Company A, 28th Infantry Regiment, at Vancouver Barracks, Washington. The28th Infantry's first action and first campaign streamer was won in December 1901, while suppressing the Philippine Insurrection. As one of the original units of the 1st Infantry Division, the 28th Infantry Regiment was the first American Unit committed conflict in World War I.

For its gallantry in action, the 28th Infantry was twice awarded the "Croix de Guerre", France's highest military decoration, and won the family crest and name, "The Lions of Cantigny." During World War II, the 28th Infantry, as part of the 8th Infantry Division, participated in the campaigns of Normandy, Northern France, and was later re-assigned to the 1st Infantry Division. The Battalion arrived in South Vietnam during 1965.

During the year 1967, eighty-five "Black Lions" gave their lives in Vietnam.

Appendix C

59 soldiers Killed in Action as a result of the Battle of Ong Thanh

1. Clifford Breeden - age 22, single, Hillsdale, MI, Alpha

2. Jerry Lancaster - age 20, single, Lebanon, TN, Alpha

3. Ralph Carrasco - age 20, single, Phoenix, AZ, Alpha

4. Wesley Dodson - age 20, single, Robinson, PA, Alpha

5. Leon East - age 20, single, Ironto, VA, Alpha

6. Ray Gribble - age 24, married, Muncie, IN, Alpha

7. Larry Anderson - age 19, single, Spencer, IA, Alpha

8. Allen Jagielo - age 20, single, San Gabriel, CA, Alpha

9. Allan Reilly - age 24, married, Los Angeles, CA, Alpha

10. Richard Crites - age 23, single, Cleveland, Ohio, Alpha

11. Arturo Garcia - age 19, single, Mercedes, TX, Alpha

12. John Krische - age 20, single, West Hempstead, NY, Alpha

13. Santos Camero - age 22, single, Malaga, CA, Alpha

14. Michael Gallagher - age 21, single, New Hyde Park, NY, Alpha

15. Michael Farrell - age 19, single, New Orleans, LA, Alpha

16. Maurice Ellis - age 21, married, Asheville, NC, Alpha

17. Elwood Chaney Jr. - age 20, single, Washington, DC, Alpha

18. Anthony Familiare - age 21, single, Philadelphia, PA, Alpha

19. Walter Platosz - age 22, single, Hartford, CT, Alpha

20. Paul Fitzgerald Jr. - age 20, single, Ft. Valley, GA, Alpha

21. Olin Hargrove Jr. - age 18, single, Birmingham, AL, Alpha

22. Emil Megiveron - age 20, single, Pontiac, MI, Delta

23. Richard Jones - age 19, single, Cairo, IL, Delta

24. Gary Lincoln - age 23, single, Eaton, Ohio, Delta

25. Ronney Reece - age 18, single, Atlanta, GA, Delta

26. Kenneth Wilson - age 19, single, Clinton, NC, Delta

27. Harold Durham Jr. - age 25, single, Tifton, GA, Delta

28. Robert Nagy - age 20, single, Lorain, Ohio, Delta

29. Stanley Gilbert - age 22, single, Dexter, MN, Delta

30. Gary Barker - age 20, single, Garden Grove, CA, Delta

31. Robert Fuqua Jr. - age 19, single, Mansfield, Ohio, Delta

32. Michael Miller - age 20, single, Mt. Pleasant, FL, Delta

33. Joe Crutcher - age 21, single, Winter Park, FL, Delta

34. Donald Adkins - age 19, single, Gretna, VA, Delta

35. Melesso Garcia - age 20, single, Watsonville, CA, Delta

36. 2nd Lt Andrew Luberta - age 24, Chicago, IL, Delta

37. Theodore Thomas Jr. - age 21, single, Houston, TX, Delta

38. Luther Smith - age 34, married, Miami, FL, Delta

39. Joe Moultrie - age 20, married, St. Stephan, SC, Delta

40. Jackie Bolen Jr. - age 19, single, Ury, WV, Delta

41. Steven Ostroff - age 20, Sun Valley, CA, Delta

42. Edward Dye - age 20, single, Wellston, Ohio, Delta

43. Melvin Cook - age 20, single, Salem, OR Delta

44. Jackie Shubert - age 23, single, Jacksonville, FL, Delta

45. Daniel Sikorski - age 20, single, Milwaukee, WI, Delta

46. Captain James Blackwell Jr. - age 26, married, Evansville, IN, HHC

47. Sgt Major Francis Dowling - age 38, married, Cooperstown, ND, HHC

48. Joe Lovato Jr. - age 20, single, Lubbock, TX, Delta

49. Pasquala Tizzio - age 20, single, New York, NY, HHC

50. SP5 Verland Gilbertson - age 40, single, Banning, CA, HHC

51. SFC Eugene Plier - age 37, married, Sheboygan, WI, HHC

52. Garland Randall - age 26, married, Houston, TX, HHC

53. Sgt James Larson - age 20, single, Mauston, WI, HHC

54. LTC Terry Allen - age 38, married, El Paso, TX, HHC

55. Jack Schroder - age 20, married, Clay Center, NE, Delta

56. Major Donald Holleder - age 33, married, Webster, NY, HHC

57. Joseph Booker -age 22, single, Richmond, VA, Delta, *Died October 18*

58. Archie Porter - age 25, married, Cameron, WV, HHC, ***Died October 21***

59. Willie C. Johnson Jr. - age 26, married, Savannah, GA, Alpha, **Died *November 9***

Appendix D

Presumptive Conditions for Agent Orange

AL Amyloidosis

A rare disease caused when an abnormal protein, amyloid, enters tissues or organs

Chronic B-cell Leukemias

A type of cancer which affects white blood cells

Chloracne (or similar acneform disease)

A skin condition that occurs soon after exposure to chemicals and looks like common forms of acne seen in teenagers. Under VA's rating regulations, it must be at least 10 percent disabling within one year of exposure to herbicides.

Diabetes Mellitus Type 2

A disease characterized by high blood sugar levels resulting from the body's inability to respond properly to the hormone insulin

Hodgkin's Disease

A malignant lymphoma (cancer) characterized by progressive enlargement of the lymph nodes, liver, and spleen, and by progressive anemia

Ischemic Heart Disease

A disease characterized by a reduced supply of blood to the heart, that leads to chest pain

Multiple Myeloma

A cancer of plasma cells, a type of white blood cell in bone marrow

Non-Hodgkin's Lymphoma

A group of cancers that affect the lymph glands and other lymphatic tissue

Parkinson's Disease

A progressive disorder of the nervous system that affects muscle movement

Peripheral Neuropathy, Early-Onset

A nervous system condition that causes numbness, tingling, and motor weakness. Under VA's rating regulations, it must be at least 10 percent disabling within one year of herbicide exposure.

Porphyria Cutanea Tarda

A disorder characterized by liver dysfunction and by thinning and blistering of the skin in sun-exposed areas. Under VA's rating regulations, it must be at least 10 percent disabling within one year of exposure to herbicides.

Prostate Cancer

Cancer of the prostate; one of the most common cancers among men

Respiratory Cancers (includes lung cancer)

Cancers of the lung, larynx, trachea, and bronchus

Soft Tissue Sarcomas (other than osteosarcoma, chondrosarcoma, Kaposi's sarcoma, or mesothelioma)

A group of different types of cancers in body tissues such as muscle, fat, blood and lymph vessels, and connective tissues

The VA assumes that certain diseases can be related to a Veteran's qualifying military service. They are called"presumptive diseases."- http://www. publichealth. va. gov/exposures/agentorange/conditions/

Appendix E

Neurological and Psychiatric Symptoms of Agent Orange

Gastrointestinal :

Loss of appetite, nausea, vomiting, diarrhea, jaundice, liver inflammation, vomiting blood, abdominal pain, gastric hyperplasia, gastric ulcers

Genitourinary:

Stones, burning, bloody urine, dribbling, brown urine, bladder discomfort, kidney pain

Neurological:

Tingling, numbness, dizziness, headaches, twitching, sleep apnea, in coordination, unnaturally, drowsy, loss of sensation in extremities

Psychiatric:

Violent, irritable, angry, severe depression, suicide, manic, tremulous, memory loss, loss of concentration, severe personality changes

Metabolic:

Fatigue, rapid weight loss, spontaneous fever, chills

Cardiovascular:

Elevated blood pressure, blood deficiency

Skin:

Chloracne, rash, increased sensitivity to heat or sun, altered skin color, loss of hair, brittle nails

Cancer:

Tumors, live, lung, testicular, ear duct

Family:

Miscarriage's child deaths, birth defects: cleft palates, open eye, kidney abnormalities, enlarged liver, enlarged head, club foot, missing or abnormal fingers or toes, missing or abnormal reproductive organs

Endocrine:

Enlarged male mammary glands, excessive milk flow from nipples, decreased sexual drive, difficulty maintaining erection

Visual:

Blurring, burning

Hearing Loss:

Respiratory:

Difficulty or painful breath, shortness of breath

Agent Orange Symptoms and Effects

http:// www. hadit. com/vaclaimslibrary/agentorangesymptoms. htm

Appendix F

PTSD Checklist

1. <u>Nightmares</u> - Combat- related nightmares during a typical week or month.

2. <u>Flashbacks</u> - If you have flashbacks, how frequently do these occur?

3. <u>Numbness</u> - Feeling numb and have difficulties feeling much of anything.

4. <u>Loss of Interest</u> - Many veterans have much less interest in their family, friends, and other activities that were once important to them.

5. <u>Loss of Closeness</u> - You don't feel close to almost no one.

6. <u>Jumpiness</u> - Many veterans are jumpy, hyper alert and startle easily

7. <u>Sleep Disturbances</u> - You may not be able to get to or stay asleep or have nightmares.

8. <u>Guilt</u> - Guilt about having survived when others did not or feel guilty.

9. <u>Concentration Problems</u> - Trouble concentrating or remembering things where you did not have this problem

before being in the service.

10. Avoidance - Avoid activities that remind them of combat-related events or Vietnam.

11. Self -Medication - Many veterans suffer from drug and alcohol problems to try to block out Vietnam-related feelings, thoughts, nightmares, or to get to sleep.

12. Loss of Control - You may be concerned about the possibility of losing your temper (or have done so in the past) and are worried having violent conduct on your part.

13. Depression - You are continually depressed, particularly about your ability to function normally.

14. Isolation - Many veterans are totally isolated in their communities and have few if any friends and few contacts with other people other activities.

U. S. Department of Veterans Affairs, PTSD Checklist (Major PTSD Symptoms)

http://www. ptsd. va. gov/professional/assessement/adult-sr/ptsd-checklist. asp

Sources

_____

_____

Books

Anthony, Michael, Civilized, A Young Veteran's Memoir, Pulp, 2016

Barham, Peter, Forgotten Lunatics of the Great War, New Haven, Yale University Press, 2004

Boyle, Richard, Flower of the Dragon, The Breakdown of the U. S. Army in Vietnam, Rampart Press, 1972

Butler, Curtis, PTSD My Story, Please Listen, Author House, 2010

Conrad, John, Among the Walking Wounded: Soldiers Survival and PTSD, Dundurn, 2017

Cortright, David, Soldiers in Revolt, GI Resistance During the Vietnam War, Anchor Press/Doubleday, 1975

Dawe, Ronald and Schroder, William, Soldier's Heart, Close-up Today with PTSD in Vietnam Veteran, Praeger Security International, 2007

Finkel, David, Thank You for Your Service, New York, Picador, 2013

First Infantry Division in Vietnam, 1 May1967 - 31 Dec 1968, Volume II

Forrest, Emma, Your Voice In My Head, A Memoir, New York, Other Press, 2011

Handy, Marla, No Comfort Zone, Mocassa Press, 2010

Herr, Michael, Dispatches, Everyman's Library, 2009

Hogue, Charles, Once A Warrior Always A Warrior, Lyons Press, 2010

Johnson, James, Combat Chaplain: A Thirty-Year Vietnam Battle, University of North Texas Press, 2015

Lembcke, Jerry, The Spitting Image: Myth, memory, and the Legacy of Vietnam, New York, University Press, 1998

Liebert, John and Birnes, William, Wounded Minds, Skyhorse Publishing, 2013

MacGarrigle, George, Taking the Offensive, October 1966 to October 1967, Center of Military History, United States Army, 1968

Mahler, Michael, Ringed in Steel, Presidio Press, 1986

Maraniss, David, They Marched into Sunlight, War and Peace, Vietnam and America, October 1967, Simon & Schuster, 2003

McWilliams, John, The 1960s Cultural Revolution, Greenwood Press, 2000

Morris, David, The Evil Hours, A Biography of Post-Traumatic Stress Disorder, Houghlin Mifflin Harcourt Publishing, 2015

Muscan, Mary, What Nurses Know, PTSD, Demos Health, 2012

Najavits, Lisa, Seeking Safety, Guilford Press, 2002

Neu, Charles, E, America's Lost War Vietnam: 1945-1975, Wheeling, Illinois, Harlan Davidson, Inc, 2005

Paulson, Daryl and Krippner, Stanley, Haunted by Combat, Rowman & Littlefield Publishers, 2007

Percy, Jennifer, Demon Camp, A Soldier's Exorcism, Scribner, 2015

Raja, Sheela, Overcoming trauma and PTSD, New Harbinger Publications, 2012

Rawson, Andrew, The Vietnam War Handbook, US Armed Forces in Vietnam, The History Press, 2008

Rochester, Stewart, and Kilay, Fredrick, Honor Bound, American Prisoners of War in Southeast Asia 1961-1973, Annapolis, Maryland, Naval Institute Press, 1999

Ronnau, Christopher, Blood Trails, The Combat Diary of a Foot Soldier in Vietnam, Presidio Press, 2006

Scranton, Roy, and Gallagher, Matt, Fire and Forget, DaCapo Press, 2013

Seahorn, Janet & Anthony, Tears of a Warrior, A Family's Story of Combat and Living with PTSD, Team Pursuits, 2017

Shay, Jonathan, Achilles in Vietnam, Combat Trauma and The Undoing of Character, Scribner, 1994

Shelton, James, The Beast Was Out There, The 28th Infantry Black lions And The Battle of Ong Thanh, October 1967, Cantigny First Division Foundation, 2002

Singelin, Guillaume, PTSD, First Second, 2019

Small, Melvin, Antiwarriors, The Vietnam War and The Battle For America's Hearts And Minds, Scholarly Resources Inc. , 2002

Soloman, Andrew, The Noonday Demon, An Atlas of Depression, New York, Scribner, 2001

Tibbetts, Terry, A Spartan Game, The Life and Loss Of Don Holleder, iUniverse, 2011

Tick, Edward, War and the Soul, Theosophical Publishing House, 2005

Vonnegut, Kurt, Slaughterhouse-five, Dial Press, 2009

Whitney, Catherine, Soldiers Once, Da Capo Press, 2009

Wilcox, Fred, Waiting for An Army To Die, The Tragedy Of Agent Orange, Vintage Books, 1983

Periodicals

Time, A Sudden Meeting, page 36, October 27, 1967

Newsweek, Ambush of the Black Lions, page 44, October 30, 1967

Notes from Jim Kasik, 2/28th Bravo Company Commander 1967, Operation Shenandoah II, Oct 7 to Oct 17, 1967

Operation Billings from 2/28th Bravo Company website - freepages. military. rootsweb. ancestry. com/~realmccoy/billings. html

Annual 2nd Bn 28th Inf History, Black Lions, Republic of Vietnam, 1967

Interviews: (Survivors from Battle of Ong Thanh)

1) 34 Interviews done by the U. S. Army Center of Military History, Historical Resources Branch.

2) Interviews conducted by Mike Dinkins: Joe Costello & Edward Grider.

3) Interviews conducted by Fred Kirkpatrick:

(Alpha Company): Ken Anderson - 1st platoon, Alpha Company, Mike Arias - 1st platoon Sgt RTO, Alpha Company, David Duncan - 3rd platoon, Alpha Company, Paul Kay - FO, Alpha Company, Thomas Mullen - 3rd platoon leader, Alpha Company, Jerry Price - RTO (up) for Captain George, Alpha Company Commander, Jose Valdez - 1st Sgt, Alpha Company

(Delta Company): Clarence Barrow -1st Sgt, Delta Company, Astor Caudill - 2nd platoon, Delta Company, John Fowler - 2nd platoon, Delta Company, Robert Gomez - 2nd platoon medic, Delta Company, Mike Kotowski - 3rd platoon, Delta Company, Greg Landon - 1st platoon, 3rd squad RTO, Delta Company, David Laub - RTO for 3rd platoon leader, David Stroup, Delta Company, Bill McGath - 3rd platoon, Delta Company,Paul Scott - RTO (dn) for Company Commander, Clark Welch Delta Company, Mike Troyer - 2nd platoon, Delta Company,